EDITED BY **ADAM BOXER**
SERIES EDITOR **TOM BENNETT**

THE research ↓**ED** GUIDE TO

EXPLICIT & DIRECT INSTRUCTION

AN EVIDENCE-INFORMED GUIDE FOR TEACHERS

First Published 2019

by John Catt Educational Ltd,
15 Riduna Park, Station Road,
Melton, Woodbridge IP12 1QT

Tel: +44 (0) 1394 389850
Email: enquiries@johncatt.com
Website: www.johncatt.com

ISBN: 978 1 912906 37 6

Set and designed by John Catt Educational Limited

WHAT IS researchED?

researchED is an international, grassroots education-improvement movement that was founded in 2013 by Tom Bennett, a London-based high school teacher and author. researchED is a truly unique, teacher-led phenomenon, bringing people from all areas of education together onto a level playing field. Speakers include teachers, principals, professor, researchers and policy makers.

Since our first sell-out event, researchED has spread all across the UK, into the Netherlands, Norway, Sweden, Australia, the USA, with events planned in Spain, Japan, South Africa and more. We hold general days as well as themed events, such as researchED Maths & Science, or researchED Tech.

WHO ARE WE?

Since 2013, researchED has grown from a tweet to an international conference movement that so far has spanned six continents and thirteen countries. We have simple aims: to help teaching become more evidence-facing; to raise the research literacy in teaching; to improve education research standards; and to bring research users and research creators closer together. To do this, we hold unique one-day conferences that bring together teachers, researchers, academics and anyone touched by research. We believe in teacher voice, and short-circuiting the top-down approach to education that benefits no one.

HOW DOES IT WORK?

The gathering of mainly teachers, researchers, school leaders, policymakers and edu-bloggers creates a unique dynamic. Teachers and researchers can attend the sessions all day and engage with each other to exchange ideas. The vast majority of speakers stay for the duration of the conference, visit each other's sessions, work on the expansion of their knowledge and gain a deeper understanding of the work of their peers. Teachers can take note of recent developments in educational research, but are also given the opportunity to provide feedback on the applicability of research or practical obstacles.

CONTENTS

FOREWORD:
IT'S THE WAY YOU TELL THEM

Among the most maddening things that new teachers face is a dilemma that is so vast and absurdly obvious that it is hard to even give it a name: 'What is the best way for me to teach?' – along with the quandaries 'How can I get the students to follow my instructions?' and 'Do I know enough about this?' These are the fundamentals that grip us. It will come as a huge surprise to non-teachers (and still some surprise to many teachers) that answering these questions is frequently not a large part of a teacher's formal induction into the profession.

What they do frequently get is a series of well-meant suggestions of how to build elaborate activities that are designed primarily to engage or excite – such as games or 'fun' activities – or tasks designed to satisfy some other, often social or cultural objective – teaching them how to work well in groups, be creative, be tolerant etc.

I say 'well-meant' because they are, but this model of professional practice is as far removed from the ideal as homeopathy is from open-heart surgery. The teacher is still left unsure if the knowledge or skills content of the lesson was received, transmitted or understood memorably, unless they are assessed. But even so, what then? Repeat the same pedagogical leap of faith?

But there is an entire study of this process which, in a feat of absurdity extraordinary even for education, is often absent from teacher preparation: explicit instruction, and its cousin, direct instruction. This is the studied craft and the structured scientific investigation into how we impart information and content in ways that are as optimally memorable as possible. This, surely, should be at the heart of the teacher's project, whatever one's subject or phase.

Teachers should be rightly suspicious when they're told what 'research proves'. In order for that to be the case, it's necessary for a significant portion of the teaching community to be reasonably research literate – enough to generate a form of herd immunity – both in content and methodology. Then, they can reach out to and engage with research which can assist their decision making. I say 'assist' carefully.

That doesn't mean making their decisions for them; that doesn't mean it's a trump card. Teachers need to interact with what the best evidence is saying and translate it through the lens of their experience. If it concurs, then that itself is significant. If it clashes, then that's an interesting launch platform for a conversation. Teaching is not – and can never be – a research-based or research-led profession. Research can't tell us what the right questions to ask are, nor can it authoritatively speak for all circumstances and contexts. That's what human judgement, nous and professional, collective wisdom is for. But it can act as a commentary to what we do. It can expose flaws in our own biases. It can reveal possible prejudices and dogma in our thinking and methods. It can assist bringing together the shared wisdom of the teaching community. It can act as a commentary to what we do. It can and should be nothing less than the attempt to systematically approach what we know about education, and understand it in a structured way.

Teaching can – and needs to be – research informed, possibly research augmented. The craft, the art of it, is at the heart of it. Working out what works also means working out what we mean by 'works', and where science, heart and wisdom overlap – and where they don't.

Here, Adam Boxer has assembled a superb collection of some of the education sector's pre-eminent voices in this field, both in the academic arenas and in the field of practice. At researchED we have always championed this duality, because we believe that only through the interaction of science and craft can we arrive at the most probable strategies for teachers to use in the only place they matter – in rooms full of children.

One day it will seem strange that any educator did not know this topic intimately, or were not able to quote these commentators critically at the beginnings of their careers. One day. That day hasn't come yet. Until then, I believe that this book is an invaluable overview of some of the most interesting and practical voices engaged in this field's great conversation. I hope you find it useful, interesting, and thought-provoking.

Tom Bennett
Founder, researchED
Series editor

INTRODUCTION

When I first qualified to teach, I considered myself a 'social constructivist' in my approach to teaching and to learning. In this regard, I was quite unremarkable, and completely in line with the educational orthodoxy. I believed that there was a specially privileged place for knowledge which students had generated themselves and that somehow information which was directly provided for students by teachers was less well embedded in their consciousness. In this vein, I felt comfortable in having met the teaching standards, and had no self-doubt at all when it came to ticking off the sub-clause in teachers' standard 2 stating that teachers must 'demonstrate knowledge and understanding of how pupils learn and how this impacts on teaching' (Department for Education, 2011). As such, my students completed many open inquiries, research tasks and discovery-based activities. They wrote definitions for themselves, gleaned vital information from posters stuck around the room and spent lots of time teaching each other. I don't think I was particularly remarkable in this regard: my practices were never challenged and feedback was always about surface details of the lessons, not about the philosophy that underpinned them.

A few years into my career, I came across the Sutton Trust's *What Makes Great Teaching?* document (Coe et al., 2014). Within the report, the authors summarised foundational and robust research findings that would best support teacher quality. One section was headed as 'ineffective practices', and true to its title, went on to list a number of teacher activities that were either unlikely to lead to improved learning or would actually harm its progress. Some of these I knew about already: I knew that learning styles were bunk, that lavish praise could be counterproductive and that grouping students by ability was precarious at best. What I was not prepared for was the simple statement that an example of an ineffective practice was to 'allow learners to discover key ideas for themselves', with the authors arguing that:

> Enthusiasm for 'discovery learning' is not supported by research evidence, which broadly favours direct instruction (Kirschner et al., 2006). Although learners do need to build new understanding on what they already know, if teachers want them to learn new ideas, knowledge or methods they need to teach them directly.

In less than 50 words, a foundational plank of my educational philosophy had been removed. I had made claims to being an 'evidence-informed' teacher, and thought that my practices were well supported by the literature. This was the first serious challenge to my teaching I had received.

I followed the report's citation to Kirschner et al.'s 2006 article, which reviewed the evidence from the cognitive sciences regarding how minimal guidance during instruction was significantly less effective than fully guided, teacher-led instruction. From there, I was slowly introduced to the arena of the cognitive sciences and stronger models of human thought and condition than I had previously used to satisfy the second teachers' standard.

It is inevitable that some research findings will be better known than others. Some ideas spread and gain traction; others struggle to find their feet. In recent years, well-established findings like cognitive load theory and retrieval practice appear to be making ground, hopefully to the betterment of thousands of students across the world. The aim for policy makers, leaders and teacher trainers should be to push the highest impact strategies further into the public consciousness, to occupy a 'Goldilocks zone' of being both effective and well known. The topic of this book, Engelmann's programme of Direct Instruction, unfortunately sits in the exact opposite of this: an *anti*-Goldilocks zone of being the least known strategy with a frustratingly large impact. How can it be that a teaching style with such an incredibly high impact can be known to so few? Kris Boulton's opening chapter brings this dilemma into sharp relief. Tracing the fascinating history of Project Follow Through – the study that would pit Engelmann's programmes against other teaching styles, – he shows convincingly how there are both methodological and ideological structures in place which have prevented widespread acknowledgement of Direct Instruction's strength. He cites Engelmann describing how those opposing his programmes brought their objections to the corridors of power, utilising political routes to halt rolling them out. Though history will judge those involved, Direct Instruction lives on, and its lessons can and should be learnt by teachers across the world.

Direct Instruction is a specific programme with scripts, focused resources and teaching sequences planned to the most minute of details. Triangulating evidence from Project Follow Through, the cognitive sciences and other large-scale research projects, Greg Ashman describes the major features of Direct Instruction and compares it to more expansive teaching styles like 'explicit instruction' or 'direct instruction' (with no capitals). Ashman convincingly shows that the overwhelming weight of evidence supports fully guided instruction – where the teacher is in complete control of the learning process.

It is clear as time goes on and the evidence base becomes better disseminated that more and more teachers are turning to an explicit instruction model of teaching – a model that relies heavily on themes from Direct Instruction and other evidence-based programmes.

This book is therefore not just about Direct Instruction as a specific programme designed by Engelmann. This is a book about how teachers in the UK can, and are, being inspired by Direct Instruction in their own practice. In our context it is vital that we borrow key elements from Direct Instruction in thinking about how we can best tailor instruction to the needs of our students. A teacher who employs explicit instruction in their teaching will most likely be borrowing from research in the cognitive sciences, process-product studies and Project Follow Through. And whilst an entire library could be written on the influence of each of those evidence bases on explicit instruction, this volume aims principally to expose the thread that leads from Engelmann to explicit instruction.

As such, one crucial feature of Direct Instruction is its use of examples and non-examples. In complementary chapters, Tom Needham and Gethyn Jones show the power of examples in revealing meaning to students. Sometimes, a technical definition, though correct, can 'darken' understanding and prevent students from latching onto a concept. Using examples to explain concepts allows students to actively make inferences about the commonalities between the examples and, through inference and extrapolation, move towards nuanced and rich appreciations. Non-examples are shown to be incredibly powerful in promoting hard thought and showing the boundary conditions within which a concept holds true. Using examples is powerful for students, and it also forces teachers to appreciate the nature of the concepts they are due to be teaching and how they are best encapsulated and defined.

Naveen Rizvi continues the theme by deploying another technique from Direct Instruction called covertization. She shows how not only the careful sequencing of examples but also the teacher's active use of cues, step-by-step algorithms and deliberate guidance can slowly build students up to becoming competent solvers of open problems. In this way she makes clear a thread that runs throughout this book – a thread that points to the end goal of explicit instruction: building students whose teaching has been so thoughtful and well sequenced that they are able to rapidly progress to a point at which they no longer have need of the teacher who at first guided them so supportively.

Sarah Cullen's chapter puts the above into practice through her invocation of fading. We must always begin teaching with as much support and guidance as possible but with time, practice and feedback, we begin to rely on that support less and less, eventually reaching the culmination of all that work, where students, in her words, 'take their first flight … a thrilling moment in teaching'. Cullen's essay serves as a rallying call to teachers to help their students achieve the joy and satisfaction of mastering, internalising and applying a complex body of knowledge.

Cullen's consideration of fading across years, terms and lessons is our first real taste of how insights from Direct Instruction can inform curricular planning at all levels. In a wide-ranging chapter, Amy Coombe and Lia Martin apply lessons from Direct Instruction to all levels of an ongoing attempt to teach writing. They show how deep thought from a wide perspective allows us to ensure that we are properly covering and imparting the fundamentals of the writer's craft to our students, without tacitly leaving holes or incomplete understandings in their knowledge. Bursting with practical examples, they perceptively include findings from Doug Lemov's seminal *Teach Like a Champion*, findings which serve to buttress a Direct Instruction-inspired theory of teaching.

A common criticism of both Direct Instruction and explicit instruction is that they are boring and disengaging. Nothing could be further from the truth, with Project Follow Through showing that Direct Instruction was the most effective teaching strategy not only for students' knowledge and understanding, but also for their 'affective' scores – how much they enjoyed the subject. Sarah Barker traces the underlying psychology behind the feelings of satisfaction and mastery that accompany expert teaching and instruction and urges us to think about motivation as a feeling that develops over time in tandem with feelings of competence, mastery and self-assurance. We cannot control the emotions and feelings our students bring to class. But we can control how well they are taught, and we can hope that through expert teaching they grow as active appliers of the knowledge imparted and take strong steps on the path to long-term motivation and enjoyment.

Though this book mostly deals with Direct Instruction's influence on explicit instruction, this of course isn't to say that Engelmann's programmes themselves aren't highly valuable, and Hannah Stoten describes a viable approach for school leaders to actually go about implementing a full Direct Instruction programme. In such contexts it's vital that leaders are aware of the potential obstacles that will need to be overcome. Sometimes those obstacles are prosaic – people naturally being resistant to going against the way things have always been done – but sometimes they are more culturally weighty, revolving around issues of standards and expectations. She argues that accepting the potential of Direct Instruction programmes also involves accepting and promoting higher standards of behaviour, engagement and focus than the ones we may have grown used to.

Summer Turner builds on all that has come so far by describing how Engelmann's work relates to an increasingly popular curricular discourse. Elegantly weaving together philosophical ideas from prominent curriculum theorists with the more functional tools of Direct Instruction, Turner shows how the steady build up of knowledge throughout a course of studies enables students, and especially the most disadvantaged, to flourish. In order to achieve this, not only must the instruction be flawlessly sequenced at a micro level, but the technical set-up of the curriculum must be flawless in its macro sequencing and opportunities for regular revisiting of past content. Summer's chapter should serve as a springboard for thought when planning a curriculum. However, it is obviously not a complete guide to how to build a Direct Instruction curriculum and should not be used as such. We hope that, in conjunction with this book series' sister volume *The researchED Guide to the Curriculum*, educators will gain crucial knowledge and conceptual tools by which to frame their curricular discussions.

Engelmann was not just an expert educator; he was a socially minded ideologue. He believed that all students could learn and that the historic use of ineffective teaching methods walked hand in hand with a gradual erosion in society's beliefs of what young people from the hardest backgrounds could achieve. John Blake's chapter explores why it is that such young people tend to fall behind and what systemic, societal and pedagogical causes lie beneath this widespread phenomenon. He argues convincingly that the route to a more socially mobile student body must come via a curriculum centred on powerful knowledge and implemented by teachers inspired by Engelmann's techniques.

I noted at the outset that Direct Instruction sits in an anti-Goldilocks zone. In an education system obsessed with impact, intervention and improvement, its omission from teacher training courses, CPD events and the general professional discourse is striking. researchED is proud to be at the forefront of teaching teachers the most powerful techniques that decades of educational discourse and training have failed to convey. Learning lessons from Direct Instruction, the greatest educational intervention ever designed, is a vital part of that process.

References

Coe, R., Aloisi, C., Higgins, S. and Major, L. E. (2014) *What makes great teaching? Review of the underpinning research.* London: The Sutton Trust. Retrieved from: www.bit.ly/3182O2d

Department for Education (2011) *Teachers' standards: guidance for school leaders, school staff and governing bodies*. London: The Stationery Office. Retrieved from: www.bit.ly/2YrExSY

Kirschner, P., Sweller, J. and Mayer, R. (2006) 'Why minimal guidance during instruction does not work: an analysis of the failure of constructivist, discovery, problem-based, experiential, and inquiry-based teaching', *Educational Psychologist* 41 (2) pp. 75–86.

Author bio-sketch:

Adam Boxer teaches chemistry at a school in North London. He writes about science education, cognitive science and evidence-based practice and is an active member of #CogSciSci, a grassroots collective of more than 600 science teachers looking to support each other in implementing science teaching based on the cognitive sciences.

WHAT WAS PROJECT FOLLOW THROUGH?

BY KRIS BOULTON

In 1966, seven children sat in front of a teacher and blackboard. As they waited, they jiggled in their seats; some kicked their feet back and forth, while others stretched and raised their hands before lowering them again. Finally, the teacher started, and asked them a question: 'What's eight plus two?' *Ten!*, they all called out together. Twenty seconds later and they'd answered five questions like this. The teacher wrote 38 + 14 on the board, in column form, and asked them what to do. One explained, and then *No!* – all the children cried out as the teacher deliberately followed the instruction incorrectly. Three of them leapt out of their seats to correct the mistake.

Fifteen minutes later, and the teacher wrote $C + M = R$ on the board. 'What if I want to end up with C?' the teacher asked, and all seven children explained $C = R - M$. 'What if I want to end up with M?' $M = R - C$ came the response.

Then, 'I really don't expect you to be able to get that. Now this is too tough – but we'll try it anyway.'

'Do these together.'

$$A - B = 0$$

$$A + B = 10$$

An abortive 'two plus two' is suggested, before 'five plus five' is quickly offered.

Finally, 'One more? Getting tougher!'

This time the teacher wrote:

$$A + B = 14$$

$$A - B = 2$$

They sat together in silence for 90 seconds. Some children stared at the floor, some counted on their fingers, some rubbed their eyes, until finally, a meek voice suggested 'eight and six?'

That these seven children progressed in 20 minutes from evaluating 8 + 2 to solving simultaneous equations would be remarkable in any situation. When you learn that these children were only four years old, it borders on the incredible. But happen it did, and stories like this one have been repeated over and over in schools following programmes of instruction created by Siegfried Engelmann, an American psychologist turned educationalist, the man who would go on to become the developer and senior programme designer of Direct Instruction.

Engelmann created the video that depicts the above event (Engelmann, 2013) in response to criticism he'd received – some of it personal,[1] some of it critical of the instructional practices taking place in the schools he supported. They were described by critics as hot houses that pressured children (Engelmann, 1992, p. 1) and that would inevitably crush their innate interest, creativity and will to learn. Yet in this video, nothing to that effect can be observed.

Establishing Project Follow Through

The ultimate opportunity for Engelmann's methods to prove themselves came in 1967, under US President Lyndon Johnson. Project Follow Through was established, a research programme that would continue for nearly three decades, from 1967 to 1995, at a total cost of about a billion dollars (Grossen, 1995). Its stated goal was to find 'the most effective practices' (Hill, 1981, p. 20), and to do this, it pitted nearly two dozen different instructional programmes against one another in a 'horse race,' to see which came out top. These most effective practices would then be rolled out nationally, 'clearing the air of rhetoric about what works and what doesn't' (Engelmann, 1992, p.3).

These instructional programmes worked with children from the moment they entered state education up until the end of third grade (Year 4 in England) and they varied wildly in their design. For example, the Direct Instruction programme specified a precise instructional methodology, and its intention was to succeed in teaching basic skills in reading, arithmetic, and language. The language development approach, on the other hand, specified no teaching procedures, and instead focused just on the *existence* of some kind of language support for Spanish-speaking children, with a positive emphasis on the child's native language and culture. The Tucson early education model (TEEM) and cognitively oriented curriculum both

---

1. As early as the second paragraph in *War Against the Schools' Academic Child Abuse*, Engelmann explains that 'sociolinguists took shots at it on the grounds that we did not ... even know the difference between "thinking and speaking".'

stressed child-centred learning, with the curriculum determined by the child's interests. The latter was derived from Piagetian theory, and had children schedule their own activities, with teachers trained to function as catalysts rather than providers of information (Watkins, 1997, pp. 26–28).

The most significant analysis of programmes' relative success came ten years after it started, in 1977. It evaluated 13 of the 22 programmes that made up Follow Through, and included over 200,000 children. The analysis was conducted by Abt Associates, who grouped the 13 programmes three ways, depending on their stated aims.

The first group were called the **basic skills models** and included Direct Instruction. These emphasised the teaching of fundamental skills in reading, arithmetic, spelling and language. The second group were called the **cognitive-conceptual models** and included TEEM and cognitively oriented curriculum. This group focused on 'learning to learn' and problem-solving skills. The third and final group were called the **affective-cognitive models**, which focused on development of academic self-concept, positive attitudes towards learning, and then 'learning to learn'.

These three groupings served as a framework for evaluating the programmes. Children were tested for acquisition of basic skills, for cognitive and problem-solving skills, and for their attitudes towards school, towards learning, and their associated academic self-image.

They were assessed using a suite of ten tests, seven of which were taken from the Metropolitan Achievement Test elementary level.[2]

The expectation was for programmes to perform well in their respective domains, so each type of programme might serve a different purpose. Basic skills programmes would have the most impact on basic skills, for example, while the affective programmes would have the most impact on academic self-concept.

---

2. To test basic skills, four tests called Word Knowledge, Spelling, Language and Math Computation were used. To test problem solving and broader cognitive ability, the four tests used were Raven's Colored Progressive Matrices, Reading, Math Concepts and Math Problem Solving. Finally, two tests were used to assess for academic self-concept: the Coopersmith Self-Esteem Inventory, and the Intellectual Achievement Responsibility Scale (IARS).

This isn't, however, what the analysis showed.

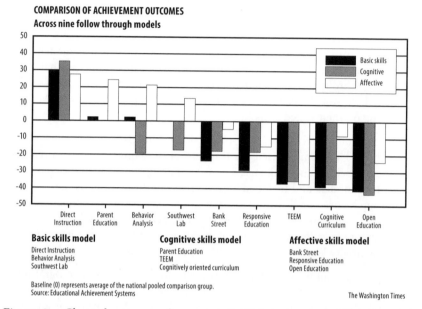

COMPARISON OF ACHIEVEMENT OUTCOMES
Across nine follow through models

Figure 1 – Chart showing performance of children in nine Follow Through programmes, compared with a control group

Direct Instruction outperformed every other programme in all three categories of assessment. Amongst the headline findings published by Abt Associates were:

1. Models that emphasize basic skills succeeded better than other models in helping children gain these skills.

2. Where models have put their primary emphasis elsewhere than on the basic skills, the children they served have tended to score lower on tests of these skills than they would have done without Follow Through

3. No type of model was notably more successful than any other in raising scores on cognitive-conceptual skills, meaning that no overarching category was successful, and specifically, none of the individual cognitive programmes were either. But the Direct Instruction programme, taken on its own, was successful in raising scores on cognitive conceptual skills.

4. Models that emphasise basic skills produced better results on tests of self-concept than did other models.

Abt Associates weren't the only people who performed analysis of the Follow Through data. House et al. (1978, cited in Watkins, 1997), Bereiter and Kurland (1981, cited in Watkins, 1997), and Kennedy (1978, cited in Watkins, 1997) also produced independent analyses – and each time, Direct Instruction came out top by a large margin.

What went wrong? – Methodology

So, what happened? Where's all the Direct Instruction in our schools? Why are we not all trained in the approach? Why do our institutions of teacher education still focus on Piagetian ideas, and naturalistic developmentalism?

Follow Through wasn't originally conceived as an experiment. The administration of Lyndon Johnson had 'declared a full scale war on all poverty', and part of that had been the Head Start programme, a social services programme targeting disadvantaged pre-schoolers, and aiming to close the gap between them and their more affluent peers by the time they started school. Head Start was perceived as successful, but there was also a perception that its effects dissipated in the years after it finished. So, a new programme was conceived to 'follow through' on Head Start, by providing similar ongoing social support once children were in school.

It was declared that $120 million would be made available for the first year of the programme, but budget cuts pulled this back to only $15 million. It was impossible to provide social support on the scale imagined with such a small budget, so to save it, Follow Through was reconceived as a large-scale experimental programme.

Nothing of this kind had ever been attempted before. Many of the administrative and experimental designs were new, and yet it needed to be in place and ready to go on an extremely short timescale, a matter of months. In addition, on the books it was never officially changed from being a social services programme to a research programme, leading to administrative confusion about its intentions, and further frustrating the experimental design. For example, some goals were pursued that were in conflict with good experimental design, in the hope of proving the social good of the programme so that a larger budget, closer to the original, would be released the following year. There was even confusion around whether Follow Through programmes were required to provide social services – such as food and dental provision – to children and parents.

Other problems included a lack of specification for programme design, explaining why a programme like Direct Instruction might have precise specifications for teacher procedures, while another, like *Language Development Approach* has none. Some children also ended up experiencing three years of a *Follow Through* programme, while elsewhere in the country they would experience four years, due to differences in school entry ages between school districts in the US.

The most frequently cited design flaw, however, was the lack of random assignment of the programmes to schools. Instead, schools could opt into a programme of their choosing.

So, while the aim of Follow Through was to identify the most effective instructional practices and disseminate them throughout the country, critics of Direct Instruction – the 'most effective instructional practice' according to the Follow Through analysis – used methodological imperfections such as these to argue that the data in support of DI could not be trusted, and therefore Direct Instruction should not be promoted over alternative programmes.

What went wrong? – Ideology

There are people who claim that the methodological criticisms of Follow Through, while sometimes valid, have often been overemphasised because the real motivation of its critics is an *ideological* disagreement with the project's most successful programme, Direct Instruction. For example, Watkins (1997, p. 58) cites 'conflict with existing philosophies', as a key obstacle to rolling out Direct Instruction: 'These are ... examples of the way in which professional educators have responded to the **challenge of their philosophies** that the Follow Through results constitute' (emphasis added).

Similarly, from Watkins: 'When early evaluation results **were not favourable**, the evaluation was criticized' (Watkins, 1997, p. 78; emphasis added). This led to an alternative analysis being privately commissioned by the Ford Foundation, 'the House critique', before the final results from Abt Associates were even concluded (Watkins, 1997, p. 35).

The foreword to *Why Education Experts Resist Effective Practices*, a paper written by Douglas Carnine, makes the point that 'in education, research standards have yet to be standardized, peer reviews are porous, and practitioners **tend to be influenced more by philosophy than evidence**' (Carnine, 2000; emphasis added).

In regards to the design of the programmes being tested by Follow Through, Bonnie Grossen wrote: 'The models developed by the academics consisted largely of **general statements of democratic ideals and the philosophies of famous figures**, such as John Dewey and Jean Piaget. The expert preschool teacher's model [Siegfried Engelmann and Direct Instruction] was a set of lesson plans that he had designed in order to share his expertise with other teachers' (Grossen, 1995; emphasis added).

Following the aftermath of Follow Through, Englemann wrote, 'Heavy duty lobbying efforts warned politicians against telling communities that their 'child development' Follow Through model was a bust. After all, the parents loved it and thought it was great for their kids; the district loved it and didn't really care whether it was good for their kids so long as it brought in the federal dollars' (Engelmann, 1992, pp. 5–6).

A recent meta-analysis published in 2018 also observed that 'despite the very large body of research supporting its effectiveness, DI has not been widely embraced of implemented. In part, this avoidance of DI may be fuelled by the current **popularity of constructivism** and misconceptions of the theory that underlies DI' (Stockard et al., 2018; emphasis added).

This is not so dissimilar from the concerns of educationalist E.D. Hirsch, who in his 1999 book *The Schools We Need, and Why We Don't Have Them* dedicated an entire chapter to a 'Critique of a Thoughtworld', unpicking the ideology that in his view holds back effective educational practices. When he published *Why Knowledge Matters* nearly 20 years later, nothing had changed, as he started the book by citing **developmentalism** and **child-centred practices** as among the ideas still holding back progress (Hirsch, 2016, p. 7).

Throughout the past five decades, time and time again concern has been raised regarding entrenched ideologies that prevent scientific progress in education – so much so that this obstacle itself has become the subject of books like Christodoulou's *Seven Myths About Education* (2014), and de Bruyckere et al.'s *Urban Myths About Learning and Education* (2015).

Taken together, they offer the most likely answers to the questions 'What went wrong?' and 'Why isn't DI in all our schools?' In short, on the surface, the approach doesn't appear to mesh with our pre-conceived ideologies about what schools in the 21st century should look like.

Can we really trust DI?

On the one hand, Direct Instruction was shown by Follow Through to be the most effective teaching approach – not only for fundamental skills, but for broad cognitive and problem solving skills, and also for academic self-image – what we might today call 'growth mindset'. But given all its criticism, can we really trust the conclusion of Follow Through? Can we really trust that Direct Instruction is the most effective teaching approach for learning basic skills, complex problem solving, *and* improving children's motivation and love of learning?

Critiquing the critique

Field research in a sector like education is never perfect. There are always too many variables to control perfectly, and it's near impossible to conduct a double-blind randomised control trial. This is noted by Watkins: 'Evaluation of public programs is always conducted in a context in which there are numerous parties with stakes in the continuation of the program. These stakeholders and their interests affect the way an evaluation is carried out' (1997, p. 50).

It has also been noted by E.D. Hirsch (2002) and Dylan Wiliam (2019). So, attacking Follow Through for being *imperfect* is disingenuous. Despite its flaws, it is possible to conduct field research and learn *something* from the experiment. For example, Watkins states that 'despite the design flaws noted, there were clear and consistent differences between models. The model with a preponderance of positive effects was the Direct Instruction model sponsored by the University of Oregon' (Watkins, 1997, p. 79).

Similarly, Carl Bereiter observed that the Follow Through project taught us something that previous teacher observation studies had not: that an 'ineffective teacher' could become an 'effective teacher' when they were provided a change in instructional materials and approach (Bereiter and Kurland, 1981).

Finally, what is often offered as Follow Through's biggest flaw – the lack of random allocation – is arguably one of its biggest strengths. For field research of this kind to be effective, it must be implemented by teachers and schools as the instructional designers intended. If programmes were randomly assigned to schools, and the school were then asked to implement, behind closed doors, an approach that it dislikes, then implementation is unlikely to be carried out as intended. By allowing schools to choose which programme they opted into, the probability of effective implementation was increased (Watkins, 1997, p. 22).

Corroborating research

Since Project Follow Through, research into the effectiveness of Direct Instruction has continued, and it continues to prove itself (Stockard, 2014). In addition to this body of research, there are parallels in the recommendations from teacher effectiveness studies produced by Rosenshine (2012), Lemov (2015), and Coe et al. (2014). Furthermore, a recent McKinsey analysis of the OECD PISA data revealed that student outcomes improve when classrooms have more teacher-directed methods than inquiry-based methods (Mourshed et al., 2017).

Students who receive a blend of teacher-directed and inquiry-based instruction have the best outcomes.

Point change in PISA[1] science score relative to baseline,[2]
average score increase ● or decrease ●

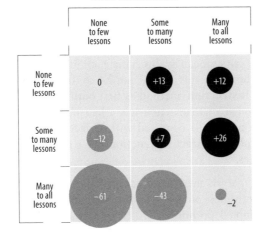

The 'sweet spot' combines teacher-directed instruction in most to all classes and inquiry-based learning in some.

[1]Programme for International Student Assessment.

[2]Statistically significant expected change in score controlling for PISA's index for economic, social, and cultural status (ESCS), public/private schools, and urban/rural location for all quadrants except for teacher-directed and inquiry-based instruction in all classes (–2), which was not significant at 95% confidence level.

McKinsey&Company | Source: *McKinsey Analysis*, OECD PISA 2015

Figure 2 – Chart showing relative success of children in classes where more teacher-directed methods are used, compared with inquiry-based methods

Each of these examples would be considered 'direct instruction' (with a lowercase d and a lowercase i) in a broader sense. Recommendations of this type are sometimes referred to as 'explicit instruction'. They share similar features to (but may be considered a 'weaker' version of) the instructional design created by Siegfried Engelmann, which by contrast has very precise instructions for how a Direct Instruction programme should be constructed (Engelmann and Colvin, 2006).

So, what happens when we look closer at the research into Direct Instruction itself, with a full-fat capital D and capital I?

23

Taking the first of two examples, in 2008, when John Hattie published *Visible Learning* about Siegfried Engelmann's Direct Instruction, he said this (emphasis added):

> Every year I present lectures to teacher education students and find that they are already indoctrinated with the mantra **'constructivism good, direct instruction bad'**.

> When I show them the results of these meta-analyses, they are stunned, and they often become angry at having been given an agreed set of truths and **commandments against direct instruction**.

> Too often, what the critics mean by direct instruction is didactic teacher-led talking from the front; this should not be confused with the very successful **'Direct Instruction'** method as first outlined by Adams and Engelmann (1996). Direct Instruction has a bad name for the wrong reasons, especially when it is confused with didactic teaching, as **the underlying principles of Direct Instruction place it among the most successful outcomes**.

Then, the 2018 meta-analysis mentioned earlier looked at 'half a century of research' into the effectiveness of Direct Instruction curricula (Stockard et al., 2018). Its results prompted prominent Dutch educational psychologist Paul Kirschner to ask publicly: 'How much more proof do we need to stop hands-on, inquiry based, constructivist education madness and get back to real effective teaching via Direct Instruction?' (Kirschner, 2018).

Logical analysis

When asking the question 'Can we really trust DI?', the previous two sections looked at the research base, first pointing out that the results of Follow Through were more robust than is sometimes implied, and second that, since the Follow Through analysis, a long history of research has corroborated its conclusion. Next, it's possible to understand and trust in the effectiveness of Direct Instruction even without that field research.

In 1982, Engelmann published *Theory of Instruction* (Engelmann and Carnine, 1982), which outlines in minute detail every facet of the design theory. Rooted in behaviourism, almost everything is predicated on just two principles: the first is that the human mind possesses the ability to recognise a particular example as an instance of a more general, abstract concept; and the second is that the mind develops the abstract generalisation after exposure to more than one example. Everything after these two principles is a systematic effort to uncover how many examples are required, of what type, and how best to present them, to form a given generalisation in the shortest possible amount of time. For example, you're able to look at an animal and understand that it is a particular instance of the more general, abstract concept 'dog'. Then, after seeing enough examples of things that are 'dogs', and things that are 'not dogs', your mind forms an abstract generalisation against which all future animals will be compared. The goal of *Theory* is to determine how many examples you need to see, and of what type, to form a mental generalisation of a specific degree of sophistication. Low-level sophistication might allow you to discriminate 'dog' from 'cat', but not from 'wolf', for example.

Unlike most instructional recommendations, it's possible to see exactly how Direct Instruction purports to function, and so it's possible to see that the mechanism of Direct Instruction makes it *very likely* to be successful, even before the research evidence is considered. It's a bit like lifting up the hood of a piano to see how each key connects to each hammer to strike each string of varying length and width. No matter how complex the composition you hear, it's not produced by a magic box; there's a clear and direct relationship between key strike and sound. And in the same way, in Direct Instruction, no matter how complex the content to be learnt, there is a clear and direct relationship between every teacher action and student outcome.

Consistency with cognitive science

The results from Follow Through are sufficiently robust that we can trust its headline conclusions. A half-century of research since then has yielded the same conclusions, and a logical analysis of the DI approach reveals precisely how and why it is effective.

Finally, to answer whether or not we can really trust Direct Instruction, we should consider the words of Kirscher et al. (2006) that 'any instructional procedure that ignores the structures that constitute human cognitive architecture is not likely to be effective'.

The design of Direct Instruction arguably did ignore the structures that constitute human cognitive architecture; it was created through an iterative process of trial and improvement. However, the final outcome is **entirely consistent with** the recommendations of cognitive science.

For example, DI programmes carefully manage cognitive load at all times. They avoid split attention and redundant information. Minimally different concepts are separated out by weeks or months in the learning sequence. Heavy use is made of the retrieval, spacing and interleaving effects. There is also frequent application of dual coding throughout the programmes.

In addition, other successful instructional approaches are found at work in DI programmes. For example, they are expressly created according to the principles of mastery curriculum design; and the principles of variation theory, popular in mathematics education, can also be found at work in DI programmes.

Direct Instruction is perhaps the only comprehensive theory of instruction that tacitly weaves together everything we know about effective instructional design from cognitive load theory, the new theory of disuse, mastery design, and variation theory.

Conclusion

Project Follow Through was the beginning, not the conclusion, of a 60-year story that has resulted in the undeniable validation of Direct Instruction as an essential body of teacher knowledge. We're now at a moment in history when two courageous claims can be made – courageous only because they point a finger at the tremendous gap between what is and what should be:

1. First, if the principles of Direct Instruction do not feature anywhere in your teaching, then you are not teaching to the very best of your capability

2. Second, all teachers, of all age groups, have a *moral imperative* to learn the principles of Direct Instruction, and how to apply them

One way to read these statements is as an accusation of our school system's failings, but there is another way to read them. We don't need an analysis of DI to know that we teachers are not realising our dream. Most of us don't walk into the classroom each day with unwavering confidence that today all 30 of our children are going to understand everything we're preparing to share with them. We already know something isn't right, and the dramatic shortfall in teacher numbers (Worth, 2018) tells this story more poignantly.

What Follow Through began was an international endeavour that, today, offers us a profound hope: there is a solution. A technology exists that can guarantee our success in teaching children, developing their minds, inspiring their hearts – every child, every day.

References

Bereiter, C. and Kurland, M. (1981) 'A constructive look at Follow Through results', *Interchange on Educational Policy* 12 (1) pp. 1–22.

Carnine, D. (2000) *Why education experts resist effective practices (and what it would take to make education more like medicine.* Washington, DC: Thomas B. Fordham Foundation.

Christodoulou, D. (2014) *Seven myths about education.* Abingdon: Routledge.

Coe, R., Aloisi, C., Higgins, S. and Major, L. E. (2014) *What makes great teaching? Review of the underpinning research.* London: The Sutton Trust.

De Bruyckere, P., Kirschner, P. A. and Hulshof, C. D. (2015) *Urban myths about learning and education.* Cambridge, MA: Academic Press.

Engelmann, S. (1992) *War against the schools' academic child abuse.* Garden City, NY: Halcyon House.

Engelmann, S. (2013) *Direct instruction archive – arithmetic* [Video]. Association for Direct Instruction, 23 April. Retrieved from: www.bit.ly/2YEjlxS

Engelmann, S. and Carnine, D. (1982) *Theory of instruction: principles and applications.* Eugene, OR: NIFDI Press.

Engelmann, S. and Colvin, G. (2006) *Rubric for identifying authentic Direct Instruction programs.* Eugene, OR: Engelmann Foundation.

Grossen, B. (1995) 'The story behind Project Follow Through', *Effective School Practices* 15 (1) pp. 1–7.

Hattie, J. (2008) *Visible learning: a synthesis of over 800 meta-analyses relating to achievement.* Abingdon: Routledge.

Hill, P. T. (1981) *Follow Through and the problem of federal education programs.* Santa Monica, CA: RAND Corporation.

Hirsch, E. D. (2002) 'Classroom research and cargo cults', *Policy Review* [Online], 1 October. Hoover Institution. Retrieved from: hvr.co/2ySQ9nJ

Hirsch, E. D. (2016) *Why knowledge matters: rescuing our children from failed educational theories.* Cambridge, MA: Harvard Education Press.

Kirschner, P. A. (2018) [Tweet] 22 July. Retrieved from: www.bit.ly/2ZVIkcz

Kirschner, P. A., Sweller, J. and Clark, R. E. (2006) 'Why minimal guidance during instruction does not work: an analysis of the failure of constructivist, discovery, problem-based, experiential, and inquiry-based teaching', *Educational Psychologist* 41 (2) pp. 75–86.

Lemov, D. (2015) *Teach like a champion 2.0: 62 techniques that put students on the path to college.* Hoboken, NJ: John Wiley & Sons.

Mourshed, M., Krawitz, M. and Dorn, E. (2017) *How to improve student educational outcomes: new insights from data analytics.* New York, NY: McKinsey & Company. Retrieved from: mck.co/2H1w7M8

Rosenshine, B. (2012) 'Principles of instruction: research-based strategies that all teachers should know', *American Educator* 36 (1) pp. 12–19, 39. Retrieved from: www.bit.ly/2Kw17qg

Stockard, J. (ed.) (2014) *The science and success of Engelmann's Direct Instruction.* Eugene, OR: NIFDI Press.

Stockard, J., Wood, T. W., Coughlin, C. and Khoury, C. R. (2018) 'The effectiveness of Direct Instruction curricula: a meta-analysis of a half century of research', *Review of Educational Research* 88 (4) pp. 479–507.

Watkins, C. L. (1997) *Project Follow Through: a case study of contingencies influencing instructional practices of the educational establishment.* Cambridge, MA: Cambridge Center for Behavioral Studies.

Wiliam, D. (2019) 'Teaching not a research-based position', *Tes* [Online], 30 May. Retrieved from: www.bit.ly/2YS4AHh

Worth, J. (2018) 'The UK's teacher supply is leaking…and fast', *Tes* [Online], 28 June. Retrieved from: www.bit.ly/2MkXBRl

Author bio-sketch:

Kris Boulton is an international teacher trainer and education writer. He spent five years working as a maths teacher in inner-city schools and was an Associate Tutor and a Director at Teach First. He is currently Director of Education at Up Learn, an online platform that provides A level study and revision courses powered by cognitive science and AI.

EXPLICIT TEACHING

BY GREG ASHMAN

A professor lectures a group of undergraduates. A facilitator explains a key concept to a group of students who are conducting an inquiry together. A primary school teacher asks students to chant the phoneme that corresponds to the grapheme she has written on the board. A football coach monitors her students as they perform drills, intervening from time to time. Who would you describe as using *explicit teaching*?

In a sense, it is up to you. There is an argument for describing all of these approaches as explicit; and even if there were not, as Humpty Dumpty explains in Lewis Carroll's *Through the Looking Glass*, 'When I use a word, it means just what I choose it to mean – neither more nor less.' And yet, when we use the terms *explicit teaching, explicit instruction* or *direct instruction*, we are borrowing from an educational tradition that possesses a unique relationship with evidence, and so it is worth being aware of what that evidence shows.

For instance, when the government of the Australian state of Victoria lists 'explicit teaching' as one of ten 'high-impact teaching strategies' (State of Victoria Department of Education and Training, 2017), what exactly does it mean? Our professor's lecture is out because the authors state that they are not referring to an 'uninterrupted monologue'. The authors also write about guiding student practice, something that our professor seems unlikely to engage in during a lecture.

From roughly the 1950s to the 1970s, *process-product* studies were a highly active area of inquiry among educational researchers. In some senses, process-product research is still being conducted, with the Programme for International Student Assessment (PISA) and its use of survey data fitting partly into this tradition.

In process-product research, different elements of the teaching and learning process (such as whether the teacher explains a lesson's learning objectives to the students) are captured, and correlations are then sought between these behaviours and gains in student performance on assessments. These are not true experiments because the different factors are not controlled by an experimenter and students are rarely randomly allocated to classes. This makes it harder to draw firm conclusions than it would be from an experiment. For instance, suppose we found that explaining the learning objectives was correlated with higher student gains. We could not know whether the former caused the latter. It may be the case that all teachers have been instructed to share learning objectives; the more conscientious teachers heed this instruction and it is actually their conscientiousness that causes the higher student gains. We could potentially dream up any number of alternative explanations.

Essentially, this is the same problem faced by researchers when they seek to determine whether smoking causes lung cancer or whether human activity causes climate change. Yet in both of these cases, a scientific consensus has emerged that there *is* a direct cause. When we have enough correlational evidence from a wide enough range of studies, we reach a point where it becomes overwhelming.

In 1984, Jere Brophy and Thomas Good reviewed the previous decade's worth of process-product research (Brophy and Good, 1984). They identified a number of factors associated with greater student gains, some of which may seem like common sense.

For instance, students learn more when they are taught by businesslike teachers who focus on academic content and activities. More-effective teachers also maximise student engagement with these activities by utilising rules and procedures and by possessing 'withitness' – regularly monitoring the classroom, scanning the room and nipping problems in the bud before escalation (Good and Brophy, 2008) – when interacting with students. Perhaps a little more surprisingly in an age where we have come to fetishize struggle (see e.g. Warshauer, 2015), effective teachers obtain a very high success rate when students answer the teacher's questions or complete activities – about 75% for questions and 90–100% for seatwork activities. This is achieved by breaking the learning down into manageable chunks. There is therefore a tension between maintaining a brisk pace with ambitious content goals and ensuring a high level of success. There is a tightrope for teachers to walk.

A key characteristic of the more effective classrooms is described by Brophy and Good as 'active teaching' (Brophy and Good, 1984). This involves students being taught or actively supervised rather than being left to work on their own and includes frequent phases where the teacher 'presents information and develops concepts through lecture and demonstration', gives practice examples, monitors progress on assignments before assigning independent work and provides feedback and reteaching where necessary. Crucially, 'the teacher carries the content to the students personally rather than depending on the curriculum materials to do so'. It is perhaps this active component, involving demonstrations and examples, which has led to this model of teaching being described as 'explicit'.

Barak Rosenshine draws on much of the same research in his influential 'Principles of Instruction' paper, although he perhaps wisely declines to name the overall approach (Rosenshine, 2012). This is unlikely to be an accident because Rosenshine has previously written about the ambiguity of the term 'direct instruction' when used to describe these principles (Rosenshine, 2008). According to Rosenshine, when people use the term 'direct instruction', they may be referring to something akin to the findings of the process-product research, but they may also be referring to any kind of teacher-led instruction at all or perhaps even using the term pejoratively to connote authoritarian lecturing where students sit 'passively' – an uninterrupted monologue.

However, the alternative term for direct instruction – explicit teaching – hardly fares any better. It should be clear from the findings of Brophy and Good – findings echoed by Rosenshine – that we are talking about an *entire process*. Explicit teaching is not just the episode within a lesson when information is presented; it involves chunking content into small components, guiding students' initial attempts at working with that content and gradually releasing control into more open activities as students gain mastery. It is a teaching model that progresses from 'I do' to 'we do' to 'you do'.

This form of teaching therefore cannot somehow sit as an event that occurs within the currently popular inquiry-based learning model because it is a model in its own right. Moreover, the principles of explicit teaching directly contradict those of inquiry-based learning. Inquiry-based learning is difficult to define, but it usually involves students pursuing answers to some prompt, question or hypothesis for themselves, with varying amounts of teacher support (Pedaste et al., 2015). This is antithetical to explicit teaching because something, no matter how small, has been left for the students to figure out for themselves.

If you wish to describe a short episode of information giving that takes place within an inquiry-based learning model as 'explicit teaching', then you are free to do so. However, you cannot point to process-product research in support of this approach. Indeed, there is substantial evidence that models such as inquiry-based learning are less effective than explicit teaching (Kirschner et al., 2006).

Given what we have learned from process-product research about teacher effectiveness, it is sometimes hard to understand how models such as inquiry-based learning can become so popular. It is as if football coaches suddenly decided that the best way to train players was to tether each of them to a small rhododendron because it would cause them to struggle more. However, it is worth examining some of the reasons that are advanced against an explicit approach.

Returning to the process-product research, it is possible to question the validity of the product (i.e. gains in student performance on academic tests). There are those who argue that this is an artificial metric or that academic tests assess knowledge and students don't need knowledge anymore in the age of Google. As Andreas Schleicher, the OECD's director for education and skills, suggests, 'the things that are easy to teach and test have also become easy to digitise and automate. Google knows everything. We are no longer rewarded based on what we know, but how we use our knowledge' (Schleicher, 2019).

This sets up an interesting dichotomy between merely knowing something and being able to use that knowledge. Yet, there is very little evidence that one can be divorced from the other. Sometimes, these applications of knowledge are described as if they are distinct skills or capabilities that can be generally applied and trained independently of particular content. However, it appears that our ability to think critically about a particular topic is intimately related to our knowledge of that topic (Willingham, 2007).

To maintain the dichotomy between knowing facts and applying knowledge, we have to suppose that explicit teaching is only useful for drilling students in facts. In reality, explicit teaching can and is used for teaching a wide range of knowledge and skills, including what we might consider to be higher order abilities such as reading comprehension and mathematical problem-solving strategies (Rosenshine, 2009; 2012).

Project Follow Through was the largest educational experiment ever conducted. It was originally intended to be an addition to the US government's Head Start programme, but after funding was dramatically cut by Congress, it turned into an experimental study (Evans, 1981). Different groups of researchers developed elementary school programmes and then the outcomes of these programmes were compared. There was one clear winner, a programme labelled by its developers as *Direct Instruction*. The Direct Instruction model developed for Follow Through was a particular form of explicit teaching designed by Siegfried Engelmann and associates that made use of scripted lessons (Engelmann et al., 1988). Direct Instruction was not only more effective at developing students' basic skills than alternative models, it was also more successful at developing the ability to comprehend written passages or solve mathematical problems (Bereiter and Kurland, 1981).

We can look to a completely different source to see a similar pattern. The Organisation for Economic Cooperation and Development (OECD) run a battery of academic assessments every three years on samples of students from a range of different countries. In 2015, they added an assessment of 'collaborative problem solving'. Those countries that had performed well in the more traditional academic subjects also featured highly in the collaborative problem-solving assessment. For instance, Singapore and Japan topped both the league table for science performance and the league table for collaborative problem solving (OECD, 2016; 2017). So there really is little evidence that explicit teaching is only effective for basic kinds of learning and that we need something different in order to develop supposedly higher order skills.

In the years since the heyday of process-product research, we have continued to discover more about effective teaching and the related issue of how the human mind learns. As we do, we begin to develop a cognitive explanation for the effectiveness of explicit teaching.

One view of how the mind learns, cognitive load theory, has been developed by John Sweller and colleagues. Cognitive load theory models the mind as consisting of a very limited working memory and an effectively limitless long-term memory. Explicit teaching mitigates the limitations of working memory by providing students with new concepts in small chunks in a controlled manner. Alternatives to explicit teaching, such as inquiry-based learning, risk overwhelming students with a large amount of information. One of the key experimental discoveries of cognitive load theory is the 'worked example effect', where relative novices learn more by studying worked examples than by solving equivalent problems, demonstrating the value of instructional guidance. Critically, this effect reverses for experts who learn more from problem solving than from worked examples. This adds weight to the explicit teaching model with its gradual release of control from the teacher to the students (Sweller et al., 2011).

Cognitive load theory also posits that schema – webs of connected facts and concepts – that are held in long-term memory can circumvent the limitations of working memory. It really does pay to have a grasp of the fundamentals because you can bring these effortlessly to mind when you need them. Knowledge is what you think *with*. You cannot outsource it to the internet.

Explicit teaching also deploys what contemporary learning scientists would refer to as 'retrieval practice' and 'spaced practice'. The former involves regularly testing students and the latter involves regularly reviewing material taught earlier in a course. The evidence for both kinds of practice can be found directly from many replicated experimental studies (Dunlosky et al., 2013).

Explicit teaching is unfairly maligned due to its misalignment with fashionable education ideology. The term itself may be abused and the evidence misrepresented. As a result, it may not be a popular approach with those in authority in schools or education systems. Yet if you want to teach effectively, the evidence suggests that explicit teaching is the best model to adopt.

References

Bereiter, C. and Kurland, M. (1981) 'A constructive look at Follow Through results', *Interchange* 12 (1) pp. 1–22.

Brophy, J. E. and Good, T. L. (1984) *Teacher behavior and student achievement. Occasional paper no. 73*. East Lansing, MI: Institute for Research on Teaching, Michigan State University.

Dunlosky, J., Rawson, K. A., Marsh, E. J., Nathan, M. J. and Willingham, D. T. (2013) 'Improving students' learning with effective learning techniques: promising directions from cognitive and educational psychology', *Psychological Science in the Public Interest* 14 (1) pp. 4–58.

Engelmann, S., Becker, W. C., Carnine, D. and Gersten, R. (1988) 'The direct instruction follow through model: design and outcomes', *Education and Treatment of Children* 11 (4) pp. 303–317.

Evans, J. W. (1981) *What have we learned from Follow Through? Implications for future R & D programs*. Washington, DC: National Institute of Education.

Good, T. L. and Brophy, J. E. (2008) *Looking in classrooms*. 10th edn. Boston, MA: Allyn and Bacon.

Kirschner, P. A., Sweller, J. and Clark, R. E. (2006) 'Why minimal guidance during instruction does not work: an analysis of the failure of constructivist, discovery, problem-based, experiential, and inquiry-based teaching', *Educational Psychologist* 41 (2) pp. 75–86.

OECD (2016) *PISA 2015 results (volume I): excellence and equity in education*. Paris: OECD Publishing.

OECD (2017) *PISA 2015 results (volume V): collaborative problem solving*. Paris: OECD Publishing.

Pedaste, M., Mäeots, M., Siiman, L. A., De Jong, T., Van Riesen, S. A., Kamp, E. T., Manoli, C. C., Zacharia, Z. C. and Tsourlidaki, E. (2015) 'Phases of inquiry-based learning: definitions and the inquiry cycle', *Educational Research Review* 14 (1) pp. 47–61.

Rosenshine, B. (2008) *Five meanings of direct instruction*. Lincoln, IL: Center on Innovation & Improvement.

Rosenshine, B. (2009) 'The empirical support for direct instruction' in Tobias, S. and Duffy, T. M. (eds) *Constructivist instruction: success or failure?*. New York, NY: Routledge, pp. 201–220.

Rosenshine, B. (2012) 'Principles of instruction: research-based strategies that all teachers should know', *American Educator* 36 (1), pp. 12–19, 39.

Schleicher, A. (2019) 'Why PISA is testing students' social and emotional skills', *The Sydney Morning Herald*, 18 May. Retrieved from www.bit.ly/2yUMAxn

State of Victoria Department of Education and Training (2017) *High impact teaching strategies – excellence in teaching and learning*. Retrieved from www.bit.ly/2YrmqRU

Sweller, J., Ayres, P. and Kalyuga, S. (2011) *Cognitive load theory.* New York, NY: Springer.

Warshauer, H. K. (2015) 'Strategies to support productive struggle', *Mathematics Teaching in the Middle School* 20 (7) pp. 390–393.

Willingham, D. T. (2007) 'Critical thinking: why it is so hard to teach?', *American Educator* 31 (2) pp. 8, 10–19.

Author bio-sketch:

Greg Ashman is a teacher and head of research at Ballarat Clarendon College, Victoria. He is a prolific blogger and has recently written a book, *The Truth about Teaching: An evidence-informed guide for new teachers.* Prior to moving to Australia, Greg worked at a number of comprehensive schools in London.

TEACHING THROUGH EXAMPLES

BY TOM NEEDHAM

DI is based around a specific conception of how learning works. The intention is to create instructional sequences where communication is faultless, and this aim can be achieved by focusing on two propositions about learners:

a. Learners have 'the capacity to learn any quality that is exemplified through examples' (Engelmann and Carnine, 1982, p. 4).

    This proposition assumes that a 'quality' is any 'irreducible feature of the example'. The assumption here is that if the learner has no sensory limitation, then they are capable of learning a quality. If we were teaching a student to understand what a dog is, there are many qualities contained within this concept (height, colour, size, etc.) and the difference between two dogs is a difference in one or many of these qualities. A teacher could demonstrate examples of tall dogs, dogs with longer hair, short dogs and innumerable other changes in qualities, each change related to the qualities in the original example. This proposition assumes that even if the changes are subtle, the learner will be able to learn what is being taught.

    The onus here is very much on the instructional designer and teacher. As Engelmann says, 'if the learner hasn't learnt, the teacher hasn't taught' (2009).

b. Learners have 'the capacity to generalize to new examples on the basis of sameness of quality (and only on the basis of sameness)' (Engelmann and Carnine, 1982, p. 4).

    If a learner is presented with a sequence of well-chosen examples about a concept, the assumption is that they will begin to mentally 'note down' what is the same about the examples, leading to the development of a mental rule. This is inductive reasoning: noting the shared 'sameness' across examples can lead to a generalized understanding of the thing that is being taught. This ability to generalize can then be tested by presenting a learner with new examples of the concept that they have not yet encountered. If the new examples also have the shared 'sameness' that the learner noted earlier, the assumption is that they will treat them the same, demonstrating generalization. If a student had been presented with a range of examples of dogs and was then tested on further examples of dogs that have a shared 'sameness', then the student will logically treat these examples the same and label them as dogs.

Teaching 'basic concepts' through examples

According to Engelmann, a 'basic concept' is 'one that cannot be fully described with other words (other than synonyms)' (Engelmann and Carnine, 1982, p. 4) and if it is to be taught properly, it will require concrete examples. Basic concepts are split into three main groups:

1. 'Non-comparative single-dimension concepts'. These would include things like 'hot', 'three', 'towards', 'under' and 'convex'. These concepts have one single defining feature. For example: 'hot' is defined solely by heat; 'towards' is defined by direction; and 'three' is defined by quantity.

2. 'Comparative single-dimension concepts'. These would include things like 'hotter', 'getting cloudier' and 'slowing down'.

3. 'Nouns'. These are multi-dimensional concepts, each one having many different features.

So why not just use words to describe the concept? Words themselves are polysemic and will mean slightly different things to each person depending on their experience and the examples of the word that they have encountered. Because of this unavoidable ambiguity, the breadth and limits of the concept will vary for each person – that is, if they have any understanding of them at all! Also, beginning with a definition may be confusing for a novice student as the words that are used to describe the concept may be abstruse or complex. This is why dictionary definitions are often little help to students with limited background knowledge. A word is merely a symbol for the underlying concept, and if examples are not presented, allowing the learner to experience the quality that the word symbolizes, the teaching sequence will not provide a solid basis for the student to understand which quality the word represents. As Engelmann explains, 'the word is not the concept and does not imply the concept to a naive person' (Engelmann and Carnine, 1982, p. 16).

How does generalization work?

DI aims to allow students 'to exhibit generalised performance to the widest possible range of examples and situations' (Engelmann, 2014, p. 76) and this can be achieved through three specific processes that accompany teaching through examples and non-examples.

1) Interpolation

Interpolation involves treating examples of a concept that lie along a continuum in the same way. Imagine you were teaching 'greyness' to a learner, and you presented examples that were broadly on a continuum of 'greyness' like this:

If the examples that you presented were found at the edges of the continuum, then if a learner was presented with a shade that came in the middle of the scale, they would logically identify it as grey.

How does this apply to the classroom?

If you were teaching the concept of 'molecules' and you presented students with two labelled examples, one that had two chemically bonded atoms and a second that had twenty chemically bonded atoms, then a student would logically treat a third example that had ten chemically bonded atoms as a molecule.

2) Extrapolation

Extrapolation involves treating small differences as being at least as important as large differences. If a small change results in an example becoming a non-example, then by extrapolation, any larger change will also result in the item being labelled as a non-example.

How does this apply to the classroom?

If you present a molecule with two of the same atoms and label it as an element and then present a second example of a molecule, this time with two different atoms, and label it as a compound, then a student will logically treat a third example that has three different atoms as a compound as well.

3) Stipulation

This process involves repeatedly presenting lots of examples that are highly similar and treating them in the same way. If the examples have too limited a range then the learner will come to think that most or all of their qualities are essential. This means that when a later example is presented that falls outside this range, the learner – through the process of stipulation – will treat it as a non-example. Usually, stipulation is something to be avoided as it limits a student's ability to generalize. Stipulation can be avoided by presenting a sufficiently wide range of examples and non-examples, perhaps through multiple sets and distributing them over time.

Communicating through examples

There are two main aims when teaching through examples – aims that seem desirable in any teaching for that matter! Firstly, the communication that the student receives should be unambiguous and precise, inducing only one possible logical interpretation. Secondly, the teaching should result in the learner being able to apply what they have learnt to a wide range of situations. When teaching through examples, we need to ensure that:

1. The examples clearly communicate the difference between positive and negative examples of the concept. This will involve precisely defining the limits and boundaries of the concept.

2. The examples demonstrate the entire range – or at least the range that you want a student to understand – of the concept.

3. There is a rigorous test that assesses the success of the teaching sequence and therefore the understanding of the student. This test should assess a student's ability to generalize and should contain items that were not taught initially.

Logical facts about presenting examples

Fact 1: It is logically impossible to teach a concept through the presentation of a single example.

Teaching through examples always requires a set of examples: it is logically impossible to present one example of a basic concept that shows only one quality. Engelmann posits that 'if you were teaching "redness", the example would have to show only "redness", not space, position, duration, shape or other identifiable non-color features. Such examples do not exist.' (Engelmann and Carnine, 1982, p. 11). The concern here is that if a learner was presented with only one example, they may associate the label of the concept with something other than the quality that you want them to focus upon.

Example:

If you were teaching 'greyness' and you presented this example, a learner could make a number of erroneous inferences because the example has many more qualities than merely its 'greyness'. A learner could infer that 'greyness' equals:

1. Things made of textiles

2. Things that are rectangular

3. A flag

4. Things attached to poles

5. Things that are in the sky

6. Things smaller than a sail

7. Things bigger than a handkerchief

This short list merely scratches the surface: one example of anything contains an indefinitely large number of qualities. Despite this, the set of concepts contained within one example will never be identical to the set within another example; if they were, they would logically be exactly the same. Because of this inherent difference between distinct examples, we are able to make observations about one example that cannot be made of another; and by manipulating the differences, we are able to rule out the irrelevant qualities that are present in one example and prevent a learner from focusing on the wrong thing.

Fact 2: It is logically impossible to present a group of positive examples that communicates only one interpretation.

If you only present positive examples to a learner, you can only *imply* the desired interpretation (Engelmann and Carnine, 1982, p. 37) as a set of positive examples can always create more than one possible interpretation. If you want to be truly precise and 'logically faultless', a sequence of examples will require non-examples in order to demonstrate the limits of a concept. As Engelmann explains:

> The smallest differences provide the greatest information. If a very small change occurs and that change is associated with a change in the label, that change must be the cause of the different label. Furthermore, since it was a very small change, the identified cause is very precise. The change marks the boundary between the positives examples and the negatives. (Engelmann and Carnine, 1982, p. 43)

Fact 3: Any sameness shared by both positive and negative examples rules out a possible interpretation.

Positive and negative examples of a concept must be treated differently: the language, label or signal used to identify a positive example must be different to the language, label or signal used to identify a negative example. If there is any sameness between positive and negative examples, then logically, this sameness cannot determine whether an example is positive or negative. This means that any sameness is irrelevant: a learner should not focus on this quality as it will not help them to discriminate between positive or negative examples of a concept.

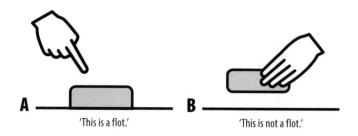

A — 'This is a flot.'   B — 'This is not a flot.'

In the above pair of examples (Engelmann and Carnine, 1982, p. 37), there are many qualities that are exactly the same in both. Here are a few:

1. Things that are grey

2. Things that are horizontally aligned

3. Things that are rectangular

4. Things that are being moved by hand

Because all of these qualities (and an indefinite number of others) are present in both positive and negative examples, these particular qualities cannot logically be the basis for defining the concept of 'flot'. Instead, the difference between the two examples is the logical basis for defining the concept.

Engelmann explains that 'for a feature to be the basis for classifying the example as positive, that feature must be present in all positives and in no negatives' (Engelmann and Carnine, 1982, p. 38).

Negative examples can be crucial for teaching. To eliminate incorrect interpretations, the teacher needs to demonstrate that specific qualities are irrelevant to the concept that is being taught. This can be done by presenting positive and negative examples that contain this irrelevant feature, inducing the learner to make a mental note of its irrelevance.

Fact 4: A negative example rules out the maximum number of interpretations when the negative example is least different from some positive example.

If a negative example is highly similar to a positive example, it will rule out more irrelevant interpretations because there will be many aspects of 'sameness' in both. All features that exist in both the positive and the negative cannot logically be the basis of the difference between them.

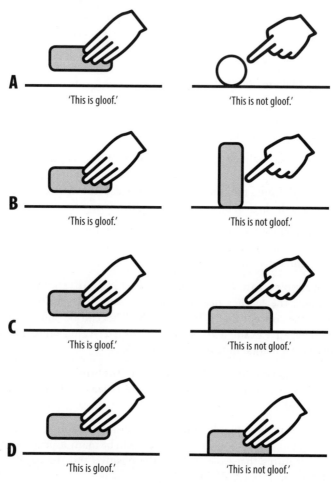

In this group of images (Engelmann and Carnine, 1982, p. 38), there are four sets of examples.

Set A creates a number of possible interpretations for the meaning of 'gloof':

1. Something held in a hand
2. Something rectangular
3. Something with corners
4. Something shaded

The negative example in set B has more of the same features as the positive example, meaning that there are fewer irrelevant interpretations that a learner could make. Unlike in set A, in set B, 'gloof' cannot mean 'something rectangular' or 'something shaded' because both of these qualities are present in the positive and the negative examples.

Only set D is 'minimally different' because there it implies that 'gloof' means 'suspended'. There is only one perceptible difference between the positive and negative example, meaning that this is what a learner will logically focus upon.

Juxtaposition principles

Here are some overarching principles about how to order, sequence and juxtapose examples. The closer that these principles are adhered to, the more likely the communication will be 'faultless' and the more likely a student will understand.

1) The wording principle

The wording principle dictates that we should use the same wording for all items in a sequence and, by precluding variance in the language used, we can minimise potential confusion and unnecessary distraction for students. While tiny or even substantial differences in wording may seem trivial to the teacher, they may have catastrophic effects for novice learners. In DI sequences, teacher scripts detail exactly what is communicated, ensuring that this principle is adhered to.

How does this apply to the classroom?

a. It may be worthwhile agreeing upon and standardising definitions for different concepts within a department.

b. When teaching concepts, try writing down what you plan to say in order to see if you are being consistent with the words that you use. Are you using several synonyms for one concept? Are you explaining an idea using unnecessarily technical language? Is all of the communication necessary? Is your explanation meandering and protracted?

c. Try to ensure that communications are not contradicted by later examples. If you define a verb as 'an action word', then this is problematic because verbs often comprise more than one word ('I *am eating* toast'/'The boys *have been watching* the news').

Here is a maths example (Watkins and Slocum, 2003, p. 78):

The wording Principle

Following the wording principle		Not following the wording principle	
$\frac{3}{2}$	$\frac{2}{3}$	$\frac{3}{2}$	$\frac{2}{3}$
The larger number is on top.	The smaller number is on top.	The larger number is on top.	In this ratio statement, the denominator is greater than the numerator.

2) The set-up principle

According to this principle, 'examples and non-examples selected for initial teaching of a concept should share the greatest possible number of irrelevant features' (Engelmann and Carnine, 1982, p. 11). This means that examples and non-examples should vary in only one way with all other aspects and features held constant. By doing this, you create a situation where interpretations and inferences are controlled, ensuring that 'only one interpretation is possible'.

How does this apply to the classroom?

This example looks at teaching present participle sentences:

Following the setup principle		Not following the setup principle	
Present participle	Avoiding gossip, Enfield is secretive and obsessed with privacy.	Present participle	Avoiding gossip, Enfield is secretive and obsessed with privacy.
Not a present participle	Enfield is secretive and obsessed with privacy.	Not a present participle	Victorian gentlemen were repressed by strict social mores.

The first column contains only one variable between the example and non-example, meaning that a learner can only make one logical inference about the meaning of 'present participle'. In the second column, there are numerous variables between the example and non-example. Although there may be many more inferences, a learner could logically infer that 'present participle' means:

a.   The inclusion of the word 'Enfield'.

b.   A sentence that is in the present tense.

c.   A sentence that is in the active voice.

3) The difference principle

The teacher and learner should treat positive and negative examples differently by using different language or labels. Carefully choosing non-examples is a crucial factor in helping students understand the 'limits or boundaries of a concept'. To understand what something is, it is helpful to comprehend what it is not. The table below (Engelmann and Carnine, 1982, p. 11) demonstrates this idea:

The difference principle

Following the difference principle		Not following the difference principle	
The line is horizontal.	The line is not horizontal.	The line is horizontal	The line is not horizontal.

The column on the left provides far more accurate and precise information as to the 'point at which an example is no longer horizontal' because both example and non-example are highly similar: the difference in orientation is only a few degrees. On the right, the examples do not provide clear information as to the delineation between horizontal and not-horizontal, the difference of orientation spanning 90 degrees.

How does this apply to the classroom?

This example looks at teaching present participle phrases:

Following the difference principle		Not following the difference principle	
Present participle	Avoiding gossip, Enfield is secretive and obsessed with privacy.	Present participle	Avoiding gossip, Enfield is secretive and obsessed with privacy.
Not a present participle	Avoiding gossip was Enfield's obsession.	Not a present participle	Victorian society was strict; gentleman were expected to conform.

In the left-hand column, the non-example is a gerund phrase (the subject of the verb 'was'). Gerund phrases are often confused with participle phrases and the juxtaposition of these two examples demonstrates why that is: they are incredibly similar. The non-example here is helpful as it gives precise information as to the delineation between 'present participle' and 'not present participle'. In the right-hand column, the non-example is massively different, making it harder for a student to ascertain the boundaries of the concept being taught.

For the difference principle to be most effective, examples and non-examples should be juxtaposed consecutively, making 'the similarities and differences most obvious' (Engelmann and Carnine, 1982, p. 11).

Here is an example:

In set B, examples 2 and 3 separate the two minimally different examples meaning that the minimal difference is not obvious and clear to the learner.

In set A, the positive and negative examples are presented consecutively, ensuring that the difference is clearly communicated to the learner. This juxtaposition of differently labelled examples ensures that the learner focuses on the minimal difference which is the only basis for a change in label (Engelmann and Carnine, 1982, p. 39). This is what Engelmann refers to as 'continuous conversion'. This is the most efficient method of communication through examples and happens when 'we change one example into the next example without any interruption of any sort' (Engelmann and Carnine, 1982, p. 34).

Here is an example sequence (p. 16):

Example		Teacher wording
		Watch my hand, I'll tell you if it gets steeper
1		It didn't get steeper
2		It didn't get steeper
3		It got steeper
4		It got steeper
5		It got steeper
6		Did it get steeper?
7		Did it get steeper?
8		Did it get steeper?
9		Did it get steeper?
10		Did it get steeper?
11		Did it get steeper?
12		Touch the line that is steeper
13		Hold up a pencil so that it is steeper than this pencil
14		Which hill is steeper? Hill A or Hill B?

In examples 1–11, the teacher is using their hand to teach the concept of 'getting steeper'. The only thing that is changing in these examples is the angle of the hand; all other qualities are kept constant. This means that the communication of 'getting steeper' is clear and precise.

Continuous conversion is logically superior to non-continuous conversion because if one example is converted into the next, only some details of an example are changed to create the next example. A number of features remain unchanged from example to example. If a change in an example leads to a change in label (from negative to positive), whatever details remain the same are irrelevant to the change in label. If a change in an example does not result in a change in label (the example staying either positive or negative), whatever details change are irrelevant to the label.

4) The sameness principle

In order to demonstrate the range and scope of a concept, we should juxtapose maximally different examples. If we were trying to teach the concept of 'dog', then we would choose examples that represent the widest possible variety of dogs. If we chose a chihuahua, an Irish wolfhound and a poodle then these examples would demonstrate that dogs come in many different shapes and sizes (Watkins and Slocum, 2003, p. 80). Although we could debate whether there are more strikingly different examples of dogs that we could use, these three have been chosen because, despite all being dogs, they are massively different. If we had merely shown different breeds of terrier, then a student may infer that any future examples that are not terriers would fall outside of the concept of 'dog'. This is what Engelmann calls 'stipulation'.

How does this apply to the classroom?

The example across the page looks at teaching students how to construct fractions that equal 1:

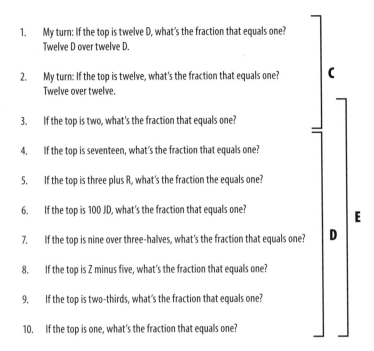

1. My turn: If the top is twelve D, what's the fraction that equals one?
    Twelve D over twelve D.

2. My turn: If the top is twelve, what's the fraction that equals one?
    Twelve over twelve.

3. If the top is two, what's the fraction that equals one?

4. If the top is seventeen, what's the fraction that equals one?

5. If the top is three plus R, what's the fraction the equals one?

6. If the top is 100 JD, what's the fraction that equals one?

7. If the top is nine over three-halves, what's the fraction that equals one?

8. If the top is Z minus five, what's the fraction that equals one?

9. If the top is two-thirds, what's the fraction that equals one?

10. If the top is one, what's the fraction that equals one?

In this figure (Engelmann and Carnine, 1982, p. 159), examples 4 to 10 are chosen to demonstrate 'sameness'. The items are maximally different, including examples that contain addition, subtraction, fractions as well as regular numbers. The intention here is to demonstrate the full breadth of the concept that is being taught.

According to Barbash (2012, p. 20):

> Most adults when asked will say a fraction is a number less than one. That's because as children we were introduced to the concept with a misleading set of examples – one-half, one-third, one-fourth. 'The biggest problem teaching higher math to kids is they don't understand fractions, so they can't manipulate them,' Engelmann says. 'After spending months working on problems where the numerator is always one, they are unable to generalize to problems like two-thirds of nine or four-thirds of twelve. They don't understand what the numbers mean.'

This example looks at teaching present participle phrases:

Following the sameness principle		Not following the sameness principle	
Present participle	Exclaiming 'The more it looks like Queer street, the less I ask', Enfield demonstrates his desire for secrecy.	Present participle	Avoiding gossip, Enfield is secretive and obsessed with privacy.
Present participle	Deliberately avoiding gossip, Enfield is secretive and obsessed with privacy.	Present participle	Disdaining gossip, Enfield doesn't ask questions of anyone.
Present participle	Enfield is obsessed with secrecy, wishing to avoid scandal and maintain his impeccable reputation.	Present participle	Eschewing gossip, Enfield explains how he never judges the actions of others.

The right-hand column only demonstrates a tiny range of possible examples of the concept. If we had merely shown these examples, then a student may infer that any differing future examples fall outside of the concept of 'present participle'. They may logically infer that present participles:

a. Always contain two words

b. Always begin with a word that ends in 'ing'

c. Always precede the subject of a sentence

d. Always begin a sentence

e. Always contain the word 'gossip'

The left-hand column demonstrates a far wider range of examples. I have deliberately inserted an example that includes a quotation as this is how students will most frequently apply these constructions. The second example begins with an adverb, preventing students from inferring the mis-rule that all present participle phrases begin with an 'ing' word. The third example has the phrase at the end of a sentence, demonstrating that these constructions are not always used at the beginning. A full sequence would contain many more maximally different examples, further broadening the scope of the concept.

5) The testing principle

After demonstrating examples and non-examples, learners should be tested to ascertain if they have acquired what is being taught. Perhaps unsurprisingly, the test should not have a predictable order or pattern. If students can game the test, then the teacher cannot draw valid inferences about student understanding. This table (Barbash, 2012, p. 81) demonstrates this idea:

Following the testing principle		Not following the testing principle	
2/4	Is this an improper fraction?	4/3	Is this an improper fraction?
3/5	Is this an improper fraction?	3/5	Is this an improper fraction?
8/5	Is this an improper fraction?	8/5	Is this an improper fraction?
48/32	Is this an improper fraction?	15/32	Is this an improper fraction?
18/12	Is this an improper fraction?	18/12	Is this an improper fraction?
6/7	Is this an improper fraction?	6/7	Is this an improper fraction?
9/3	Is this an improper fraction?	9/3	Is this an improper fraction?
		Note the alternating order: yes, no, yes, no, yes, no, yes	

Key points:

- Learners have the capacity to learn any quality through examples and to generalize to new examples.

- Teaching through examples can prevent ambiguity and subsequent confusion, ensuring that communication is faultless.

- Examples need to show the breadth and limits of the concept being taught.

References

Barbash, S. (2012) *Clear teaching: with Direct Instruction, Siegfried Engelmann discovered a better way of teaching*. Arlington, VA: Education Consumers Foundation.

Engelmann (2009) 'Instructional design 101: learn from the learners!', interview with David Boulton, *Children of the Code* [Website]. Retrieved from: www.bit.ly/2YKVVX1

Engelmann (2014) *Successful and confident students with Direct Instruction*. Eugene, OR: NIFDI Press.

Engelmann and Carnine (1982) *Theory of instruction: principles and applications*. Eugene, OR: NIFDI Press.

Watkins, C. and Slocum, T. A. (2003) 'The components of direct instruction', *Journal of Direct Instruction* 3 (2) pp. 75–110.

Author bio-sketch:

Tom Needham is Research Lead and head of English at Trinity School, Lewisham and blogs at tomneedhamteach.wordpress.com

ELECTROLYSING ENGELMANN

BY GETHYN JONES

> Effective instruction is not born of grand ideas or scenarios that appeal to development or love of learning. It is constructed from the logic and tactics of science.
>
> – Siegfried Engelmann (2011)

The communication conundrum

The philosopher Ludwig Wittgenstein began his hugely influential Philosophical Investigations (1953, §1) with a criticism of 'ostensive definitions' – that is to say, when an object is defined by pointing to it and naming it. Wittgenstein argues (1953, §28) that this method is fraught with difficulties because (1) it can only be used to define a small sub-set of words; and (2) it is open to miscommunication: if person A points at a collection of (say) two nuts and says 'Two!', what is person B (who has never seen nuts before) to infer from that? Person B could infer that 'two' meant the numeral 2, or nuts in general, or the colour, shape, or size of the objects.

Think about how confusing ostensive definitions can be. What if person A points to a pencil and says 'This is "pren".' What can person B infer about the word 'pren'?

Figure 1 Ostensive definition of 'pren' (first example)

The answer is: many, many things. The potential for miscommunication is huge. However, what if person A gives a second example?

Figure 2 Ostensive definition of 'pren' (second example)

In this case, A has given B a negative example of what 'pren' is not; however, it allows B to rule out many incorrect inferences about what 'pren' is.

Now what if person A gives person B a third example:

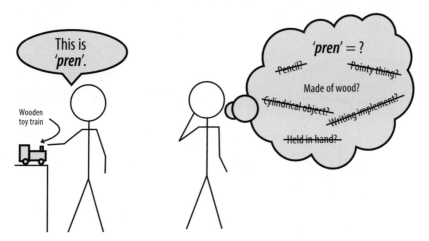

Figure 3 Ostensive definition of 'pren' (third example)

This third example allows B to (correctly) infer that 'pren' means 'made of wood'.

The point is that offering a *series of connected examples* allows us to overcome the apparent limitations of the ostensive method of definition. It allows us to navigate a pathway past Wittgenstein's conundrum.

It is analogous to that moment when you write down an incorrect answer on a crossword: the more answers that are added, the more glaringly obvious it becomes that your first guess was wrong.

Faultless communication

In *Theory of Instruction* (Engelmann and Carnine, 1982, p. 14) Engelmann proposes that everything can be taught *through the power of example*. Furthermore, he proposes that the power of example is the de facto primary mechanism by which all human beings learn.

In Engelmann's view, human beings are *inference engines* (although he does not use the term): we naturally, unconsciously and continuously infer (or attempt to infer) general rules about the phenomena we encounter. Have you ever wondered:

> Why does it always rain on me?
> Is it because I lied when I was seventeen?
>
> – Song lyric from 'Why does it always rain on me?' by Travis (1999)

It seems that we cannot help but posit causal connections between events even when, in all likelihood, there are none.

But therein lies the problem: if human beings truly are unstoppable inference engines, then surely they are just as likely to generalize false inferences from a given example-set as they are to generalize true inferences?

Of course they are – *unless*, that is, we design the series of connected examples (the example-set) with great care to eliminate (or at least minimize) the potential of drawing false inferences.

Engelmann calls such an example-set a *faultless communication* as it is 'designed to convey only one interpretation' (Engelmann and Carnine, 1982, p. 13).

Engelmann's rules for constructing faultless communications from *Theory of Instruction* (1982) are expertly outlined by Tom Needham in the previous chapter in this book and will not be treated here.

Instead, what I propose is to outline another variation or iteration on the theme of designing faultless communications which was proposed by Engelmann in his 2011 book *Could John Stuart Mill Have Saved Our Schools?*

John Stuart Mill and faultless communication

What has the 19th-century philosopher John Stuart Mill to do with Engelmann and faultless communication?

In 1843, Mill wrote *A System of Logic*, in which he attempted to codify the rules of inductive reasoning. Mill thought that this work would primarily be of interest to scientists and researchers. In essence, what Mill was trying to do was raise the status of inductive reasoning, which is often regarded as a poor relation to the more philosophically respectable deductive reasoning. He wrote (p. 4):

> In another of its senses, to reason is simply to infer any assertion, from assertions already admitted: and in this sense induction is as much entitled to be called reasoning as the demonstrations of geometry.

Sadly, *A System of Logic* received a largely unenthusiastic response from its intended audience and it languished, mostly forgotten, for well over a century.

However, when it was later accidentally re-discovered by Engelmann and Carnine, they realized that Mill's rules of induction could be applied to the realm of instruction. In fact, they 'were shocked to discover that they had independently identified all the major patterns that Mill had articulated. *Theory of Instruction* even had parallel principles to the methods in *A System of Logic*' (Engelmann, 2011).

Engelmann was so taken with the similarities between his system and Mill's that he wrote a book (*Could John Stuart Mill Have Saved Our Schools?*, 2011) where he applied Mill's formulation of the principles of induction to educational contexts.

A summary of Engelmann's analysis is outlined in the following table. Columns and text marked with an asterisk indicate my own commentary on Mill's and Engelmann's work. In other words, content highlighted with an asterisk is 'non-canonical' in the sense that I have extrapolated their ideas and examples to new situations.

The table is presented here as its sequential structure is, I believe, of great utility when designing example-sets for faultless communication.

Table 1 The Mill-Engelmann Matrix (pp. 59–61)

Name and scope of principle	Mill's statement of the principle	Engelmann's application of the principle	Simple examples	*Summary in symbolic form*	*Reasoning mode*
Direct method of agreement *Introduce concept using positive examples*	'If two or more instances of the phenomenon under investigation have only one circumstance in common, the circumstance in which alone all the instances agree is the cause (or effect) of the given phenomenon.'	'If the examples in the teaching set share only one feature, that single feature can be the only cause of why the teacher treats instances in the same way.'	Blue bird Blue car Blue sky	Examples presented to students: (a b c) is A (a d e) is A (a f g) is A Where a = 'is blue' b = 'has wings' c = 'has beak' d = 'has wheels' e = 'is a mode of transport' and so on. Students can correctly identify A when presented with new examples.	Binary (yes/no)
Method of difference *Introductory: establishing limits of concept A by explicitly considering not-A*	'If an instance in which the phenomenon under investigation occurs and an instance in which it does not occur have every circumstance in common save one, that one occurring only in the former, the circumstances in which alone the two instances differ is the effect, or the cause, or an indisputable part of the cause of the phenomenon.'	'If an example of what we want to teach and a negative example differ in only one small feature, that feature logically is the only possible basis for the teacher treating the examples differently.'	Blue bird Green bird labelled as not-blue	(a b c) is A (x b c) is not-A	Binary (yes/no)

Name and scope of principle	Mill's statement of the principle	Engelmann's application of the principle	Simple examples	*Summary in symbolic form*	*Reasoning mode*
Joint method of agreement and difference *Further developing ability of students to learn subtle differences between examples*	'If two or more instances in which the phenomenon occurs have only one circumstance in common while two or more instances in which it does not occur have nothing in common save the absence of that circumstance, the circumstances in which alone the two sets of instances differ is the effect or the cause, or an indisputable part of the cause, of the phenomenon.'	'This principle describes two sets of examples, the first of which are positive (examples of blue); and the second of which are negative (examples that are not-blue). Note that the principle of joint agreement and difference applies to any situation in which students are expected to learn a (subtle) discrimination e.g. b and b and p and q.'	• The letter 'p' • 'd' has the same shape as above, but has been rotated by 180° while flat on the page • 'b' is the same shape, but it has been flipped (as in turning over a transparent page) • 'q' has the same shape as above, but has been rotated by 180° while flat on the page	$(s\, f. \, r_1)$ is 'p' $(s\, f. \, r_2)$ is 'd' $(s\, f_2 \, r_1)$ is 'b' $(s\, f_2 \, r_2)$ is 'q' Where s = shape r_1 = Rotation position 1 r_2 = Rotation position 2 f_1 = Flip position 1 f_2 = Flip position 2	Nuanced (recognise and describe relationships, variations and transformations)
Method of residues *Non-binary responses – essentially using simple patterns to generate correct responses to more complex patterns*	'Subduct from any phenomenon such part as is known by previous inductions to be the effect of certain antecedents, and the residue of the phenomenon is the effect of the remaining antecedents.'	'For educational examples, the "part of the phenomenon that is known by previous inductions to be the effect of certain antecedents" is best conceived of as a pattern of responses. If we subduct or abstract this residue from the known antecedents, this pattern or residue is the "effect of the remaining antecedents". In other words, students have learned some of the example types that admit to a pattern, but not all the types. The instruction simply shows learners that the antecedents they haven't learned follow the same pattern as those they have learned. [...] 'The goal of instruction would simply be to arrange the examples so children learn that the more difficult examples involve the same pattern as the simple ones.'	'The learner is proficient in generating sentences that have correct subject-verb agreement for subjects with no distractors (John is walking; John and Mary are walking); but the learner makes mistakes on sentences that have subjects with distractors (The boy wearing those shoes [are] running.)'	Mill: A produces a B produces b If ABC produces abc then we can infer that C produces c. Engelmann: $a \times b = ab$ $c \times d = cd$ where $\times$ is an operation Students use simple examples to learn pattern. The pattern extracted from the examples is the 'residue'. Students gradually apply pattern to more complex examples e.g. $f \times g \times h = fgh$ $i \times j \times j = ij^2$	Nuanced and can include quantitative analysis

Name and scope of principle	Mill's statement of the principle	Engelmann's application of the principle	Simple examples	*Summary in symbolic form*	*Reasoning mode*
Method of concomitant variations *Presenting and understanding complex relationships between variables*	'Whatever phenomenon varies in any manner whenever another phenomenon varies in some particular manner is either a cause or an effect of the phenomenon or is connected with it through some fact of causation.'	'For educational applications, this method describes a pattern that involves two parallel sets of examples. Each example in the first set is transformed to a corresponding example in the second set. 'The simplest way to distinguish concomitant variation from the Method of Residues is that each item ... presents two questions, one for each of the correlated conditions.'	When the temperature increases, air expands. The temperature went from 56 to 70 degrees. • Q1 Did the temperature increase? (yes) • Q2 Did the air expand? (yes)	The state of variable a has an effect on variable b. For example, the temperature of a fixed mass of air (variable a) affects its volume (variable b) Given basic information about how the state of a affects b, students can extrapolate the pattern to a range of examples for different values of a.	Nuanced and can include quantitative analysis

Applying the Mill-Engelmann matrix in a curriculum context

One common (and not entirely unjustified) response from teachers when introduced to Engelmann's work is 'Well, I can see the value of the process when I'm teaching simple concepts like "dog" or "below", but how can I use it with (say) GCSE students?'

The remainder of this chapter will explore how the ideas could be applied to design an approach to a complex curriculum concept like electrolysis.

Applying the direct method of agreement to electrolysis

A common approach might begin with *defining* electrolysis; for example, electrolysis is the 'chemical decomposition produced by passing an electric current through a liquid or solution containing ions'.

One potential problem with this approach is that, on occasions, 'things may be made darker by definition' as Samuel Johnson memorably opined in 1791. This is a somewhat ironic comment from such a famed lexicographer whose prodigious and individual scholarship produced one of the earliest and greatest dictionaries of English in 1755. In this dictionary, the word 'network' was defined as 'any thing reticulated or decussated, at equal distances, with interstices between the intersections'.

It would seem to most of us that even one single example of an actual network would be less 'dark' than Johnson's definition. If one puts oneself in the position of a student encountering the definition of 'electrolysis' for the first time, would it be any more transparent than Johnson's definition of 'network'?

Can we provide an example-set to augment, support or perhaps even replace the definition? And what is more, can we design the example-set as a faultless communication?

We begin with the direct method of agreement, which suggests that the first example-set should be all positive examples with the structure: A = (a, b, c), A = (a, d, e) and A = (a, f, g) where A represents 'electrolysis' and the lowercase letters represent properties associated with the examples, such as the following:

Table 2 Summary of properties for direct method of agreement example-set applied to electrolysis

Letter	Property represented by the letter
a	Chemical decomposition produced by electric current
b	Electrolyte dissolved in water
c	In beaker
d	Molten electrolyte
e	In crucible
f	Electrolyte dissolved in solvent other than water
g	In graphite-lined steel electrolysis cell

In other words, the positive examples should be maximally different from each other. In fact, they should, ideally, share only one property: the property we are trying to make less 'darker by definition'.

For electrolysis, the examples presented to students as diagrams, demonstrations or video clips could be:

Table 3 The direct method of agreement applied to electrolysis

Positive example-set structure for the method of agreement	Example-set for electrolysis
A = (a, b, c)	Electrolysis of copper chloride dissolved in water chlorine given off as a gas — copper metal deposited — copper (II) chloride solution — Copper chloride is chosen as the products are more directly connected to the reactants than is the case for (say) sodium chloride.

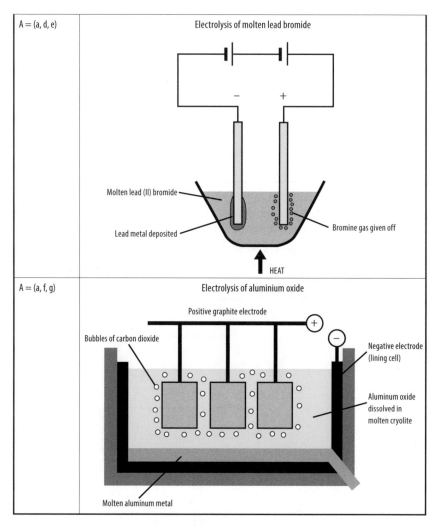

Applying the method of difference to electrolysis

The Mill-Engelmann matrix then suggests that we should next establish the limits of the concept A by explicitly considering not-A.

For electrolysis, this would be examples of electrochemistry that are not classified as electrolysis. The method of difference suggests that the examples should be as similar as possible to each other. That is to say, they should have the structure A = (a, b, c) and not-A = (d, b, c).

Table 4 Summary of properties for method of difference example-set for electrolysis

Letter	Property represented by the letter
a	Chemical decomposition produced by electric current
b	Sulfuric acid is the electrolyte
c	In beaker
d	Electrical current produced by chemical reaction in the cell

A suitable example-set for electrolysis might be:

Table 5 Method of Difference Applied to Electrolysis

Example-set structure for the method of difference	Example-set for electrolysis
A = (a, b, c)	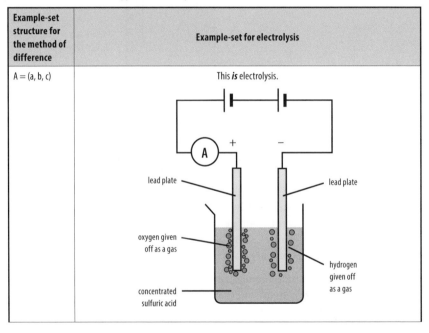

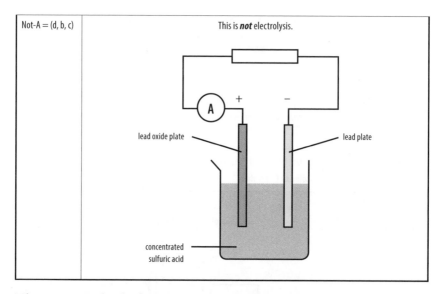

Not-A = (d, b, c)

This is **not** electrolysis.

lead oxide plate

lead plate

concentrated
sulfuric acid

The joint method of agreement and difference

Engelmann notes that designing a teaching sequence using direct instruction techniques often produces example-sets which are 'traditionally not grouped together' (2011).

It is important also to note that Engelmann does not believe that there is a single 'royal road' to design a maximally efficient teaching sequence: two designers might well produce different example-sets whilst maintaining consistency with the guiding principles of direct instruction: 'There is no single right way to achieve this efficiency; however, there are ways that are more efficient than others' (2011).

Broadly speaking, the more generalizable content should be taught first (e.g. using the method of agreement and method of difference), and the irregularities and nuances taught afterwards.

The joint method of agreement and difference invites us to construct an example-set to illustrate not only irregularities but also subtle or nuanced differences or relationships. Engelmann's example is instructive: many students struggle to discriminate between the letters 'p', 'd', 'b' and 'q' because, while the shape is constant, what varies is the shape's position and orientation in 3D space. (Note: although letters are 2D shapes, the transforms involve a 'flip' through a third dimension). Engelmann memorably suggests drawing the letter 'p' on a transparent sheet and showing how the shape is either 'P' or 'not-P' by rotating the sheet while flat on the table and flipping over (as in turning a page).

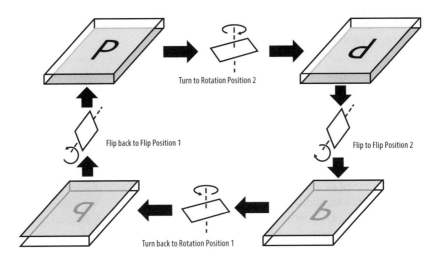

Figure 4 Applying the joint method of agreement and difference to similar letter shapes

Simpler and less-nuanced concepts than electrolysis may not require us to apply the joint method of agreement and difference at all, but complex concepts like electrolysis do.

Applying the joint method of agreement and difference to electrolysis

Let's look at an example-set showing the electrolysis of some copper compounds.

Table 6 Selected Examples of Electrolysis

Compound undergoing electrolysis	Ions involved	Product at cathode	Product at anode	Simple relationship between products and reactants?
Copper (II) chloride dissolved in water	Cu^{2+}, Cl^-	Copper metal	Chlorine gas	Yes
Molten copper (II) chloride	Cu^{2+}, Cl^-	Copper metal	Chlorine gas	Yes
Copper (II) nitrate dissolved in water	Cu^{2+}, NO_3^-	Copper metal	Oxygen gas	No
Copper (II) sulfate dissolved in water	Cu^{2+}, SO_4^-	Copper metal	Oxygen gas	No
Molten copper (II) nitrate	Cannot be done as nitrate ion will undergo thermal decomposition during the heating process			NA
Molten copper (II) sulfate	Cannot be done as sulfate ion will undergo thermal decomposition during the heating process			NA

At this stage, it should be clear to students that there are some irregularities in the process of electrolysis.

The electrolysis of copper chloride will produce copper and chlorine, whether in aqueous solution (dissolved in water) or not; there is a simple relationship between the products (copper and chlorine) and the reactant (copper chloride).

However, the electrolysis of copper nitrate is not so straightforward: copper metal will be produced but the gas produced at the anode will be oxygen and not nitrogen or 'nitrate gas' as a naive analysis would suggest.

In essence, the joint method of agreement and difference allows us to highlight where the rules of inference generated by the first example-sets shown to students should be applied with caution or not applied at all. We are showing where the generalisations we have deliberately encouraged earlier in the teaching sequence either break down or are inapplicable.

Applying the method of residues to electrolysis

A 'residue' in Mill's terminology is simply a pattern. The method of residues means identifying a pattern from a simple example-set and applying it to a different (and possibly more complex) example-set.

For example, the 'residue' or pattern we might extract from Table 6 is:

1. Ionic compounds consisting of monatomic ions (e.g. Cu^{2+}, Cl^-) can be electrolysed when dissolved in water or when molten. However, this is not true of compounds consisting of polyatomic ions (e.g. NO_3^-).

What we are saying here is that copper (II) chloride can be made to undergo electrolysis either in its aqueous (dissolved in water) state or molten state because the ions it produces are *monatomic*; that is to say, they are charged particles formed by electron transfer to and from a single atom as opposed to a complex of atoms.

$$\text{e.g. } CuCl_2 \xrightarrow{\text{\textit{dissolve or melt}}} Cu^{2+} + 2Cl^-$$

The same is not true of ionic compounds which consist of polyatomic ions:

$$\text{e.g. } CuSO_4 \xrightarrow{\text{\textit{dissolve}}} Cu^{2+} + SO_4^{2-}$$

The sulfate (SO_4^{2-}) ion will undergo thermal decomposition when heated strongly so the only way that copper (II) sulfate can be electrolysed (which requires free movement of the component ions) is by dissolving it in water

We can also surmise that:

2. The products of the electrolysis of ionic compounds consisting of monatomic ions will have a simple relationship with the original compound.

What we are saying here is that the electrolysis of aqueous copper (II) chloride will produce copper and chlorine – in other words, there is a simple relationship between the reactant compound and the products:

copper (II) chloride $\xrightarrow{\text{electrolysis in water or in molten state}}$ copper + chlorine

The same is not true of ionic compounds which consist of polyatomic ions:

copper (II) sulfate $\xrightarrow{\text{electrolysis in water}}$ copper + oxygen

At this point, students could be tested on their understanding by being asked what will happen in the following situations:

Table 7 Testing students' understanding of the 'residue'

Compound undergoing electrolysis	Ions involved	Product at cathode	Product at anode	Simple relationship between products and reactants?
Silver (II) bromide dissolved in water	Cannot be done as silver (II) bromide poorly soluble in water			NA
Molten silver (II) bromide	Ag^{2+}, Br^-			
Silver (II) nitrate dissolved in water	Ag^{2+}, NO_3^-			

The answers in the second line would be silver metal, bromine gas, and yes. The answers in the third line would be silver metal, oxygen gas and no.

Other questions could be framed using metal salts where the metals are below hydrogen in the electrochemical series. Since this treatment is intended for GCSE-level students, we will simplify this to 'metals below hydrogen in the reactivity series'.

This will be treated more fully in a later section.

'No royal road'

Some chemistry teachers may possibly disagree with some or all of the example-sets and teaching sequence outlined above. It is worth restating Engelmann's point that two different designers may choose entirely different example-sets and teaching sequences while still maintaining consistency with the principles of direct instruction and faultless communication.

The justification for choosing the example-sets and sequencing above was:

1. To cover the more generalizable content first and leave the exceptions and irregularities until later.

2. Examples were carefully chosen so that students would not encounter exceptions early on in the teaching sequence. However, given the material facts of inorganic chemistry, irregularities and exceptions soon unavoidably creep in – for example, the insolubility of some lead salts does not allow us to precisely mirror the examples given for copper salts.

3. The reason why the irregularity of the anode products of polyatomic ions was treated before the position of the metal in the reactivity series is because, in my judgement, it is a less 'difficult' irregularity in the sense that it relies only on distinguishing between monatomic ions (e.g. Cl⁻) and polyatomic ions (e.g. NO_3^-).

Engelmann's point about the principles of direct instruction producing example-sets which are 'traditionally not grouped together' is highly relevant here.

The method of concomitant variations

'Concomitant' simply means 'something that happens with something else and is connected with it'. Mill (1843, p. 271) explained this method as follows:

Whatever phenomenon varies in any manner whenever another phenomenon varies in some particular manner is either a cause or an effect of the phenomenon or is connected with it through some fact of causation.

It is helpful to think of this as a student being able to link two separate but parallel patterns to answer a question. In other words, the state of variable a has an effect on variable *b*. Given basic information about how the state of *a* affects *b*, students can extrapolate the pattern to deduce the state of *b* for a range of examples with different values of *a*.

Engelmann (2011) clarified its use:

For educational applications, this method describes a pattern that involves two parallel sets of examples. Each example in the first set is transformed to a corresponding example in the second set. The simplest way to distinguish concomitant variation from the Method of Residues is that each item … presents two questions, one for each of the correlated conditions.

In the example in Table 1, the basic information given to the students was 'When the temperature increases, air expands.' The first question is therefore to establish the state of variable *a*: 'Did the temperature increase?' If the answer is 'yes', then the student can conclude that the answer to the second question about the state of variable *b* is 'Yes – the air did expand'.

Engelmann also argues that a stronger sequence would move beyond simple yes-no responses and into comparative and quantitative responses to questions such as 'Did the temperature increase, decrease or stay the same?' and 'Did the air mass expand, contract or stay the same size?'

An example-set presented by Engelmann which features a non-causal relationship is the position of a verb changing a statement into a question. For example, 'The girls *are* reading' (statement) compared with '*Are* the girls reading?' (question). This pattern repeats with other verbs such as 'can' ('Cats can swim' vs 'Can cats swim?') and 'should' ('The students should work harder' vs 'Should the students work harder?').

Applying the method of concomitant variations to electrolysis

All the electrolysis example-sets thus far have been deliberately chosen to feature metals which are below hydrogen in the reactivity series. When we remove this restriction, new irregularities present themselves. For example:

Table 8 More selected examples of electrolysis

Compound undergoing electrolysis	Ions involved	Product at cathode	Product at anode	Simple relationship between products and reactants?
Copper (II) chloride dissolved in water	Cu^{2+}, Cl^-	Copper metal	Chlorine gas	Yes
Sodium chloride dissolved in water (high conc.)	Na^+, Cl^-	Hydrogen gas	Chlorine gas	No
Iron (II) chloride dissolved in water	Fe^{2+}, Br^-	Hydrogen gas	Chlorine gas	No

As Engelmann suggests, what we should do with this example-set is ask two questions of each item. Two suitable questions in this context would be:

1. Is the metal below hydrogen in the reactivity series?

2. Will there be a simple relationship between the products and reactants when it is dissolved in water?

If the answer to Q1 is 'Yes' then the answer to Q2 will be 'Yes': there will be a simple relationship between the product and reactants when it undergoes electrolysis when dissolved in water.

However, if the answer to Q1 is 'No' then the answer to Q2 will also be 'No'; in other words, there will not be a simple relationship between the products and reactants.

Conclusion

Consciously or unconsciously, many teachers sequence their teaching as they themselves have been taught. While some time-hallowed ways of sequencing content are the product of many generations of trial and error, others may simply be historical accident and the tacit acceptance of 'But we've always done it like this!'

In my opinion, the power of direct instructional analysis is the emphasis it puts on thinking deeply about sequencing and example-sets. Also, in spite of its reputation, it necessitates the teacher looking out through the student's eyes: *Is this content confusing? Is there a clearer way of presenting this? Is this aspect necessary? Is it better to teach B before A or A before B?*

Engelmann's application of Mill's principles of inductive reasoning to educational contexts provides, I believe, a template that teachers will be able to apply sequentially to generate example-sets that will encourage faultless communications over a wide variety of subject content.

Acknowledgements

Many thanks to Adam Boxer and Dr David Chapman for their scientific and technical advice. Any remaining errors and omissions are entirely my fault.

References

Engelmann, S. and Carnine, D. (1982) *Theory of instruction: principles and applications.* New York, NY: Irvington Publishers.

Engelmann, S. and Carnine, D. (2011) *Could John Stuart Mill have saved our schools?* Verona, WI: Attainment Company Inc.

Mill, J. S. (1843) *A system of logic, ratiocinative and inductive: being a connected view of the principles of evidence and the methods of scientific investigation* (Vol. 1). London: Longmans, Green, and Company.

Wittgenstein, L. (1953) *Philosophical investigations*. Hoboken, NJ: John Wiley & Sons.

Author bio-sketch:

Gethyn Jones is a physics teacher with over 28 years experience at the chalkface (as it used to be known). He is currently head of physics at a non-selective academy in London; is a Council Member of the Chartered College of Teaching; and blogs and tweets as @emc2andallthat.

COMMUNICATING THROUGH COVERTIZATION
CONSTRUCTING COGNITIVE ROUTINES

BY NAVEEN RIZVI

In this chapter I will focus on 'covertization', which is one element of Direct Instruction discussed in Engelmann and Carnine's *Theory of Instruction* (2017). 'Covertization' is a strategy to enable children to be taught more in less time (Engelmann, 2015).

To teach in a manner which is time efficient, we must provide learners with 'procedure(s) for developing and sequencing cognitive routines' (Engelmann and Carnine, 2017, p. 227). A cognitive routine is an action taught to a learner to help them complete complex cognitive problems.

For example, a learner is going to learn how to identify which out of two fractions is greater by placing one of the two mathematical symbols between the two fractions: < or >.

$$\frac{7}{11} \qquad \frac{3}{11}$$

A suitable cognitive routine would be to ask the learner to touch the bigger top number out of the two fractions which have the same bottom number. This small cognitive routine can eventually be internalised by the learner to then complete a fraction problem like this with no teacher guidance.

Cognitive routines can also be understood as algorithms which help learners to learn the intended fact, concept or process being communicated by the teacher. The learner will respond by either learning the intended concept or failing to do so (Engelmann and Carnine, 2017, p. 3).

One cognitive routine has been shown but a sequence of cognitive routines then becomes a structured piece of instruction. Once learners have practised several similar fraction problems by applying the set of cognitive routines then those routines become internalised. The repetitive application of the same cognitive routines allows learners to develop generalisations, identify mathematical patterns and eventually become an active seeker of information, rather than a passive receiver of information (p. 227). Learners become active seekers when the structured instruction given by the teacher requires the learners to articulate their understanding of the cognitive routine.

For example, the teacher may ask the learner: 'How do we know that we place the more-than sign between the two fractions?' This question is not asking a learner to demonstrate a cognitive routine or action but instead it is asking the learner to articulate why one fraction is bigger than the other.

Cognitive routines have helped the learners place the right symbol – not develop the ability to articulate why. This doesn't mean that strategies that help learners develop cognitive routines only teach them how to replicate a teacher's actions without any sense of why they are doing it. Instead, cognitive routines help learners internalise a set of steps to solve a complex fraction problem so that they then have the space in working memory to learn why the more-than symbol is the correct symbol.

The question asking 'How do you know...' is a 'figuring out' question where learners need to respond with a statement about sameness and differences between the two fractions. This question is not asking for a cognitive routine but instead is a question that is made accessible when a child has learnt the cognitive routines to do the action. If a child cannot place the correct symbol between the two fractions, then the question of 'How do you know...' cannot be answered by the learner.

However, if the learner can place the correct symbol between the fractions then they are more likely to answer the question successfully. Engelmann and Carnine argue that children are then able to become active seekers of information, negating a common criticism that Direct Instruction's strategies make learners passive receivers of information.

The popular 'discovery learning' philosophy, where learners are expected to 'discover sameness to concrete situations', underestimates the importance of cognitive routines, and how the repetitive practice of cognitive routines allows learners to internalise routines that help them solve complex operations (Engelmann and Carnine, 2017, p. 227).

An example of constructing cognitive routines using covertization.

Given the importance of teaching learners cognitive routines we will now look at how to develop those routines using covertization, which is 'the process of replacing the highly overtized routine with less structured routines' (p. 287).

The instruction that is given by a teacher to a learner begins as highly prompted and guided to ensure that the learner can give the desired response. The highly prompted structure to a piece of instruction can be as simple as this:

Covertization A

$$\frac{7}{11} \qquad \frac{3}{11}$$

Teacher: There are two fractions below. They have the same bottom number. They have different top numbers. Put your finger on the bigger top number.

Learner: *(touches 7)*

Teacher: Well done, you have touched the fraction with a top number of 7. Draw a circle around this fraction.

Learner: *(draws a circle around the fraction)*

$$\left(\frac{7}{11}\right) \qquad \frac{3}{11}$$

The highly prompted nature of the teacher instruction is shaping the context for the learner to respond correctly. The teacher can then guide the learner to the next action to achieve another desired response. The prompted nature of instruction enables learners to be successful during the initial teaching stages.

However, the process of 'covertization' transitions the teacher instruction from a highly prompted structure to an unprompted structure where the learner can internalise the problem-solving operation being asked of them. The teacher's directions are overt from the beginning and then become covert, guiding the learner to produce the correct response with no direction from the teacher. Therefore, the direction from the teacher will eventually become this:

Covertization B

Teacher: Place the correct symbol to show which fraction is greater.

$$\frac{7}{11} \qquad \frac{3}{11}$$

Learner: *(draws a more-than symbol between the fractions)*

$$\frac{7}{11} \; > \; \frac{3}{11}$$

Engelmann believes that applying covertization achieves a greater probability of success for all learners across the ability spectrum because when learners are unsuccessful, the fault usually lies with the instruction rather than the learners (Engelmann and Carnine, 2017, p. 3).

Covertization invites teachers to look at the wording of the instruction and consider all the points where a learner might be misled to an incorrect response, or where a learner might develop a misunderstanding of the mathematical concept being communicated.

Here is an example that is common practice in mathematics classrooms – a teacher communicating to learners what a fraction is:

Teaching example demonstrating misunderstandings conveyed to learners
Teacher: A fraction is part of a whole. A fraction has a number at the top and a number at the bottom. I will draw a list of fractions on the board.

This is a fraction
$$\frac{1}{2}$$

This is a fraction
$$\frac{1}{3}$$

This is a fraction
$$\frac{1}{4}$$

This is a fraction
$$\frac{1}{5}$$

There are several misunderstandings that a learner can extract from this teacher demonstration:

1. A fraction always has a top number of 1.

2. A fraction always has a bottom number which is never 1.

3. A fraction gets bigger when the bottom number gets bigger.

4. A fraction has a smaller top number and a bigger bottom number.

In this example there are also no examples of what a fraction is not, so learners do not learn the limits of what a fraction can be.

Here is an improved example of how to demonstrate what a fraction is:

Teaching example – corrected

Teacher: I will draw a line, and there is a number on the top and a number at the bottom. If we see a line with a number above and a number below we call it a 'fraction'. Repeat 'fraction' after me in three. Three...two...one...fraction!

Learners: Fraction!

Teacher: I will write a list of fractions and then show examples that aren't fractions.

These are fractions [delivered in sequence]

$$\frac{5}{7}$$

This is a fraction

$$\frac{7}{5}$$

This is a fraction

$$\frac{1}{5}$$

This is a fraction

$$\frac{5}{1}$$

This is NOT a fraction

$$5\frac{1}{5}$$

This is NOT a fraction

$$\frac{0}{5}$$

This is NOT a fraction

$$\frac{5}{0}$$

This is a fraction

$$\frac{5}{5}$$

Here we have communicated the following:

1. A fraction can have a smaller top number than the bottom number.

2. A fraction can have a bigger top number than the bottom number.

3. A fraction can have a top number of 1.

4. A fraction can have a bottom number of 1.

5. A fraction cannot have a whole number in front of it.

6. A fraction cannot have a top number of 0.

7. A fraction cannot have a bottom number of 0.

8. A fraction can have the same number on the top as on the bottom.

The difference between the first attempt and the corrected attempt is that in the second we have covered all the possibilities of a fraction and given examples of non-fractions.

According to the strategy of covertization, if the instructional sequence is well designed then one can ensure the highest percentage of children in the classroom are successful on the first teaching attempt. This is possible because the programme anticipates and avoids possible misteaching (Engelmann and Carnine, 2017, p. 227).

Covertization is most effective with learners who have historically been low performers. Quoting Engelmann (2015):

> If you present something new to advantaged children and they respond correctly on about 80% of the tasks or questions you present, their performance will almost always be above 80% at the beginning of the next session. In contrast, if you bring lower performers to an 80% level of mastery, they will almost always perform lower than 80% at the beginning of the next session.

> The reason for this difference is that higher performers are able to remember what you told them and showed them. The material is less familiar to the lower performers, which means they can't retain the details with fidelity needed to successfully rehearse.

Here is an example where highly prompted instructions are given by the teacher to the learner to place the correct symbol between two fractions.

Covertization C

$$\frac{7}{11} \qquad \frac{3}{11}$$

Teacher: You have two fractions. They have the same bottom value. They have different top values. Put your finger on the bigger top value.

Learner: *(touches the 7)*

Teacher: Well done, you have touched the fraction with a top number of 7. Draw a circle around this fraction

Learner: *(draws a circle around the fraction)*

$$\left(\frac{7}{11}\right) \qquad \frac{3}{11}$$

Teacher: Place two dots to the right of the first fraction. One a little above the line, and one a little below the line so they are in line with each other. Watch me. (teacher demonstrates)

Learner: *(draws two dots to the right of the circled fraction)*

$$\left(\frac{7}{11}\right)\!\!\begin{array}{c}\cdot\\\cdot\end{array} \qquad \frac{3}{11}$$

Teacher: Now to the left of 3/11, draw one dot which looks like it is in the middle of the two dots next to 7/11.

Learner: *(draws a dot to the left of 3/11)*

$$\left(\frac{7}{11}\right)\!\!\begin{array}{c}\cdot\\\cdot\end{array} \quad \cdot \quad \frac{3}{11}$$

Teacher: We are going to draw two lines using our dots. Watch me.
(draws a line from the top dot, across to the right to the single dot, and then a line from that single dot to the bottom dot on the left)

You will have something that looks like this:

$$\left(\frac{7}{11}\right) > \frac{3}{11}$$

Teacher: When both fractions have the same bottom number, this sign has a gap which always faces the fraction which has the bigger top number. The closed part faces the fraction with the smaller number – again, as long as both fractions have the same bottom number.

> **Teacher:** We place the more-than symbol between the fractions because 7 is the greater top number out of the two fractions that have the same bottom number. The first fraction is greater than the second fraction. Why do we draw the greater-than symbol?
>
> **Learner:** The 7 is the greater top number out of the two fractions that have the same bottom number. The first fraction is greater than the second fraction, so we draw the greater-than symbol.

This teacher-learner interaction involved a process of drawing a symbol between two fractions which shapes the context in which a learner can respond as easily as possible. The desired result is having a learner draw the correct symbol between two fractions. The instruction has provided a learner with the routines to draw the more-than symbol. The circling of the fraction with the greater top number of the two fractions with the same bottom number didn't help the learner achieve the intended goal, which is to draw the more-than symbol; the circling of the fraction with the larger top number has provided the child with a routine to self-check at the end. The more-than symbol will be facing towards the larger fraction, which is circled.

After circling the fraction with the greater top number, the teacher instruction is prompting the learner to draw the more-than symbol correctly. This level of specificity in instructions is essential at the initial teaching stages but eventually these specific steps are dropped because the routine becomes awkward (Engelmann and Carnine, 2017, p. 288). During the transition from highly prompted to less prompted, the learners will draw a circle around the greater fraction and use the dots to draw out the more-than symbol without the teacher having to say these specific instructions. Eventually, 'after the learner has worked many problems in the same way, this chain needs less verbal prompting' (p. 289).

For example:

Covertization D
Teacher: Draw a circle around the fraction with the greater top value.
Learner: *(draws a circle around the fraction)*
$\left(\dfrac{7}{11}\right) \qquad \dfrac{3}{11}$

The juxtaposition between the highly prompted routine in covertization example C and the less prompted routine shown in covertization example D doesn't include the first step of placing a finger on the fraction with the larger top value, or even telling the learner that the fractions have the same bottom value and different top values.

In the example of covertization C, the next attempt of transitioning to less prompted structure can begin with the following start:

Covertization E

Teacher: Place two dots. One dot, a little space below; second dot, directly below so they are in line. Watch me. *(draws a dot on the board next to a fraction, goes down by a couple of centimetres and draws another dot directly below the first one)*

Learner: *(draws two dots to the right of the circled fraction)*

$$\left(\frac{7}{11}\right) \overset{\cdot}{} \quad \frac{3}{11}$$

Teacher: Now to the left of 3/11, draw one dot which looks like it is in the middle of the two dots next to 7/11.

Learner: *(draws a dot to the left of 3/11)*

$$\left(\frac{7}{11}\right) \overset{\cdot}{} \quad \cdot \;\; \frac{3}{11}$$

Here the learner would have internalised the routine of identifying the fraction with the larger top value and circling that fraction too. The first teacher prompt would still be focusing on guiding the learner to internalise how to draw the more-than symbol. When this routine is internalised by the learner then they have learnt how to place the correct symbol between two fractions, which is the desired response from an unprompted instruction, for example:

Covertization F

$$\frac{7}{11} \qquad \frac{3}{11}$$

Teacher: Figure out the correct symbol to place between the fractions to show which one is greater.

Learner:

(circles the fraction with the greater top value)
(places two dots to the right of 7/11 and places one dot to the left of 3/11 but in the middle height of the two dots)
(draws two lines to form the more-than sign)

At the beginning, the learner is going through a fixed series of steps in order to achieve a goal. There can be instances where we can change, drop, or reorder the steps a learner takes to achieve the end goal, but there are some instances where it is not possible (Engelmann and Carnine, 2017, p. 289). Here, for example, many steps from covertization example C have been dropped:

Covertization G

$$\frac{7}{11} \qquad \frac{3}{11}$$

Teacher: Figure out the correct symbol to place between the fractions to show which one is greater.

Learner: *(places the more-than sign between the fractions)*

$$\frac{7}{11} > \frac{3}{11}$$

Teacher: How do we know that we place the more-than sign between the two fractions?

Learner: Because the 7/11 is the greater fraction: it has the greater top number when both fractions have the same bottom value. The first fraction is more than the second fraction so we use the more-than symbol.

Covertization allows the learner to go from a highly structured routine to a less structured routine because the behaviours have been internalized. The learner is also able to articulate their understanding of why the more-than symbol is the correct symbol. The last step is an example of a step that cannot be dropped or reordered.

Scheduling the transition from highly prompted instruction to unprompted instruction

The final question to ask is at what stage of the teaching process do we start transitioning learners from highly prompted to unprompted instruction?

Engelmann suggests that by overlapping procedures a teacher can 'introduce two covertization routines during the same lesson, the first of which is more highly structured than the second' (Engelmann and Carnine, 2017, p. 295). If we follow the highly prompted instruction with a similar but less prompted instruction then the learner is given the opportunity to 'perform on a less-highly structured routine' (p. 295). This allows the learner to see how the instruction is changing or progressing.

In chapter 21 of *Theory of Instruction* (p. 295), an example of an overlapping schedule is given where in each cell there is a number which states the number of examples used for a particular covertization attempt. The first covertization attempt – which is titled 'routine A' – is the first highly prompted instruction, and with more new routines introduced the less prompted the instruction becomes.

Components	Lessons								
	1	2	3	4	5	6	7	8	9
Routine A	4	2	1						
Routine B		2	4	4					
Routine C			2	4	2				
Routine D					2	5	8	8	8

The table shown states that each routine is presented on successive lessons and nearly every lesson learners are applying more than one routine. In the column titled 'lesson 2' it shows that learners are presented with two examples using routine A and two examples using routine B, demonstrating the transition from highly prompted examples to less prompted examples.

Conclusion

In summary, covertization is 'the process of replacing the highly overtized routine with less structured routines' (p. 287). A learner is given a highly structured routine to transition to a less structured routine because the cognitive routines addressed in the highly prompted instruction have been internalized. Those cognitive routines are internalized in order to then have the space in working memory to answer 'figuring out' questions.

Using a schedule where the pupils transition from a highly prompted form of instruction to a less prompted structure (where in one block of time the instruction slowly becomes less prompted) allows a learner to transition successfully to the point they can answer and complete complex mathematical problems with no assistance from the teacher.

A focus on covertization can enable pupils of varying attainment to be successful during the initial teaching stages and in high-stake assessments, but also spontaneously in future life, where the application of cogn

References:

Engelmann, S. (2015) *Teaching needy kids in our backward system.* Eugene, OR: NIFDI Press.

Engelmann, S. and Carnine, D. (2017) *Theory of instruction: principles and applications.* Revised edn. Eugene, OR: NIFDI Press.

Author bio-sketch:

Navel Rizvi is the mathematics Curriculum Advisor to the United Learning MAT. She creates Key Stage 3 and Key Stage 4 instructional materials used by over 35 schools, hundreds of teachers and experienced by thousands of pupils. The resources created use the underlying principles of Direct Instruction and Variation Theory.

FADING: REMOVING TEACHER PRESENCE IN DIRECTED TEACHING

BY SARAH CULLEN

Teachers do more than simply impart knowledge to their pupils; they enable children to understand the real beauty and joy of their subject. We want them to take the knowledge and skills we give them and really fly. This is a laudable goal that cannot be achieved immediately. Children must walk before they can run (or fly) and it is our jobs to ensure they are supported in their initial, wobbly steps, all the way through to the moment of take-off. Direct Instruction is a teaching method characterised by a strong teacher presence. As the most knowledgeable in the room, teachers closely guide learning within the lesson from start to finish. How, then, can a teaching method that so depends on instruction – on teachers leading learning and controlling the content to which pupils are exposed – foster autonomy?

Autonomy in learning occurs when a pupil can work independently – applying new knowledge and techniques to a task without the explicit help of a teacher. Reaching this point in learning requires scaffolding – structured help from the teacher that enables pupils to eventually work on their own. The moment at which a teacher steps back from the pupil and allows them to work without scaffolds – sometimes called the 'fading' stage – is a delicately balanced moment in learning. Successful fading is characterised by adaptivity and contingency of support; although it may seem a passive part of teaching, it requires a huge amount of planning, judgement and experience.

The success of Direct Instruction relies on an understanding of how memory works. In order for a student to learn knowledge or a skill to automaticity, teachers must present information in a way that can be remembered long term. Much recent research suggests that learning a new skill uses more brainpower than simply using a skill that has already been learned. Scaffolding in teaching is most effective when it is used to offer support to students at the moment they are devoting their brainpower to learning something new, and thus require the most help from a teacher. Support such as sentence starters or verbal prompts allow pupils to focus the majority of their cognitive efforts on acquiring new knowledge, and then remove that support when automaticity is reached.

The final theoretical feature in the scaffolding process requires that the teacher fade the support provided to pupils. This must only occur when internalisation of information, or automaticity, has been reached. Fading is the critical stage of this process – without the teacher's presence fading, this process of internalization cannot happen; students will instead become dependent on scaffolding rather than becoming autonomous. This moment is often described by scholars such as Fisher and Frey, in *Guided Instruction* (2010), as the moment when a teacher must 'give up control'. This phrasing implies a passivity to fading – a lessening of input and thus of effort from a teacher. The reality, as with much in teaching, involves a great deal more work than might first be apparent. The fading stage of teaching actually requires an increase in effort from the teacher. It requires a great deal of skill and attention if it is to be carried off effectively.

Fading at curriculum level – across five years

Designing a five-year curriculum enables teachers to ensure knowledge learned early on is relevant and useful to topics that are covered in later years. Ideally, pupils in older years will require less instruction and experience more automaticity in their learning. In this sense, 'fading' must be factored into curriculum planning, as well as individual lessons, to provide children with the opportunity to achieve automaticity in every subject – the final transferral of responsibility from teacher to pupil, as identified by Van de Pol et al. (2010). Explicitly planning fading in a five-year curriculum plan is essential in order to ensure academic success.

In an educationally perfect world, by planning a curriculum for younger years that is devoted to embedding key knowledge that is relevant and widely applicable, students are well equipped to spend their later years working with more independence and creativity. Early success fosters early belief; beginning years should focus on mastery of basic, essential knowledge and on low-stakes testing that allows students to quickly grow in confidence. Devoting earlier learning to establishing a 'bedrock' of knowledge (such as times tables, key historical dates or the capital cities) that will continue to be used throughout a pupil's school career means that in later years, limitations on short-term memory will be hugely reduced. Planning this 'bedrock' across five years also requires planning when to fade out revisiting that knowledge – when you need pupils to have mastered this knowledge in order to move on to the next topic more easily.

By making every new piece of knowledge count, we can avoid cramming in Years 10 and 11 in secondary. Without fading that is carefully considered and implemented only when automaticity and mastery have been fully achieved, we can end up teaching poetry in Year 7 in an isolated module, and then being surprised when we find they no longer remember how to identify a metaphor when preparing for their GCSE poetry. In this example, identification would only be the first step, anyway; mastery of what a metaphor is should then lead to being able to analyse its impact on the reader. But without a curriculum that revisits this essential knowledge and practises working with it, children are likely to struggle. A good curriculum has a clear direction, one that is driven by key knowledge and how it will be sequenced and revisited. Pupils subsequently become far more able to make connections independently and seek out patterns in their knowledge, a key step towards successful fading from the teachers as pupils reach automaticity.

The key to effective scaffolding is that it is 'gradually dismantled', as Dixon et al. state (1993, cited in Fisher and Frey, 2010) state. However, when scaffolds are removed too early, learning does not occur, as knowledge doesn't enter long-term memory. Furthermore, the learner becomes disengaged with learning in the process. 'Fading' is not only isolated to when we ask children to complete an assessment periodically without teacher input. When planning a five-year curriculum, fading must be considered in terms of when assessments should take place. Factoring assessments into the curriculum is essential, but is only useful if time is also taken to implement the results of those assessments – to decide if topics need to be revisited or not. Tests taken at the end of terms and school years are the result of some of the final fading that has taken place in classrooms.

Fading at curriculum level – across terms

'Children need opportunities to connect their prior knowledge and experiences with new information. They must be given the chance to do so through their own thought processes and through interactions with others' (Mastropieri and Scruggs, 1994). Fading provides these opportunities in an optimal way. Such opportunities allow students to use knowledge they have mastered as a basis on which to build a framework for understanding new ideas and information. Through this gradual building or scaffolding of knowledge and skills, students can be supported to move beyond rote knowledge and develop depth of understanding, fostering a love of learning – independently seeking out further material on a topic that has interested them in a lesson or simply seeking out new knowledge for the sheer joy of it.

Planning a curriculum across an academic year first requires 'advance organisers': a collection of key knowledge that will help to lay the groundwork for a topic. These are usually condensed onto a single sheet of A4 and provide a basis to refer back to when you are teaching, as well as an overview of the topic to help pupils grasp the big picture. This might include key quotations or dates, definitions and vocabulary. They are invaluable as a revision tool for pupils, as well as a method to help you to know when to begin fading – once they have mastered this information, you can fade out supports regarding it and move on to teaching new content. You can also 'fade in' to this information, terms later, to ensure scaffolding is no longer needed in relation to it.

When identifying where fading will be best placed across an academic year, allow for the fact that pupils will always find it difficult to move on to a new topic – there will feel like a step backwards in pupil ability, but this can be tempered by increased scaffolded support, and fading that takes place via low-stakes testing.

Across an academic year, assessments should gradually build in complexity to enable deeper understanding. Using well-pitched, low-stakes tests very early on in a new topic can help to offer quick success for pupils who might otherwise feel frustrated at the apparent backwards step in their ability.

Testing is key to fading, as is the time when pupils must apply knowledge without teacher support. Crucially, teachers see how much pupils have learned rather than their performance based on current practice. Allowing time to elapse between initial teaching and assessment ensures that students have embedded knowledge and that they're not just mimicking the teacher. In addition, it provides information on whether or not you need to reteach or revisit concepts – effectively fading back in again. Regular low-stakes tests and low-stakes skills practice make excellent use of the testing effect: devoting learning time to retrieving information that is being learned helps to transfer the knowledge to long-term memory (Goldstein, 2011, pp. 183–186). It is very easy to underestimate the sheer volume of simple testing required to really help knowledge stick. Weekly tests on the 'essentials' – simplified and widely relevant facts or ideas – should also be supplemented by recap questions that take place every lesson.

Weekly tests offer useful information about how often the information being learned needs to be revisited. It is best to simplify these as much as possible to minimise overload of new information and marking for teachers. Rather than providing precise grades for pupils, they should instead offer a rough idea of how well each pupil has retained the knowledge being tested. A class set of test answers should fall into three categories: those who have mastered the knowledge; those who are still making a few errors; and those who need to revisit the information until they are able to retrieve it more confidently. This testing is a form of fading: you have taught the knowledge, you have fed it into lessons and now you are asking them to retrieve it without your help. This differs from asking them to retrieve it via oral questions in lessons because it enables you to see how well the entire class has internalised this key knowledge that they will require to succeed in later stages of fading – when they have to independently apply it to their work.

This is the most basic form of fading to be found in lessons – eventually, this essential knowledge will be recalled by pupils independently, without being explicitly drawn out by the teacher via testing or questions.

Fading at lesson level

The essence of fading within everyday lessons is simple: until students can demonstrate mastery of new knowledge, they are given more assistance or support from a teacher. As the learner moves toward mastery, the assistance or support is gradually decreased in order to shift the responsibility for learning to the pupil (Larkin, 2002). Giving one modelled example followed by similar tasks of increasing difficulty is a decision teachers often take, as it is a good way to provide challenge. However, like practice, pupils will require far more modelling than you might at first suppose.

Fading should be planned into every lesson in the form of opportunities for independent application of knowledge and ideas. Fading until this point has been considered in terms of structured, pre-planned fading – when information should be revisited and when new information should be introduced, as well as how knowledge from different units and subjects can complement each other. All of this leads to the final point at which fading features in learning – within every lesson. This fading, just like the building of knowledge in Direct Instruction, is used through a variety of approaches and gradually increased.

Questioning enables a steady form of fading throughout lessons. Questions asked during new concepts should draw on knowledge that has already been established – this will enable pupils to feel secure and successful in their new work, whilst also highlighting those patterns that make curricula so much more effective and flagging the link to what they already know, helping them to make that connection. Quick-fire verbal questions are an easy way to keep past learning relevant and to help cement knowledge in long-term memory. Verbal questioning is also the simplest way to use fading in your lessons. Support can be offered via questions that include prompts ('What other play have we read that included speeches? What did we say was the effect of Antigone's speech?') but can also be used to stretch and challenge. I think of some questions as 'pulling' and some as 'pushing'. The former pull pupils towards a certain answer or idea, or attempt to coax knowledge out of them – 'What technique is being used here?'; 'Which play have we studied before that also featured celestial imagery?'; 'Is there a link between these two uses of chiasmus?'. The latter form of question attempts to push pupils out into less scaffolded or supported territory – 'How do you think Shakespeare wanted his audience to react to Lady Macbeth?' Though it may seem led by the teacher, questions that require pupils to apply knowledge to new situations is a form of fading – they prompt learners to reach new conclusions independently, a key step towards achieving automaticity. By asking questions that draw links with prior learning, you are effectively modelling for the pupils how they should use knowledge they've already learned when engaging with new texts or topics. These questions might include the activation of background knowledge, giving tips, strategies, cues and procedures. Well-designed questions will still force pupils to think and synthesise what they know and test methods, but won't ask them to stab in the dark with no sense of whether they are right or wrong.

When learners notice patterns in the knowledge you've been teaching without you using questions to draw it out, they should begin to phrase their own questions in a way that reflects this ('Are we doing it this way because it's like quadratic equations?', 'Did they believe this for the same reason the Babylonians did?'). These questions illustrate the sort of thinking that takes place when pupils are making information stick by forming connections independently. It is indicative of the fact that you have used fading effectively via questions – the pupils no longer rely on you to construct questions that reveal links in their learning. Learning thus becomes deeper, and more powerful.

One form that fading takes in the classroom is modelling. A teacher demonstrates how to complete a new task and then fades that support by having the pupil do the same as the teacher. However, this structured support is often withdrawn too early in the name of 'stretch and challenge' – teachers equate scaffolding with a lack of challenge. Letting students experience head-scratching moments is fine, but it should be in response to a question that makes use of only the knowledge they have already acquired. So often, teachers model how to respond to a set of questions, and then give pupils an entirely new, far more complex question to tackle on their own. The logic runs along the lines of 'I've shown them how to work through this kind of question – the one they do on their own should be harder or they'll be bored/simply mimicking me.' This logic is well intentioned but fundamentally flawed: leaving the hardest content for them to try on their own makes life especially hard for less-able pupils and those who have developed misconceptions from previous teaching. In addition, it makes 'giving it a go' seem doomed to failure, putting them off taking controlled risks in the future. In her blog post on using modelling in maths, Dani Quinn (2017) also points out that setting students questions that are too hard at the end of a scaffolded lesson 'adds to the perception that teachers are just refusing to tell them how to do things to be annoying. [Students] should try hard problems on their own, but [teachers] should have first equipped them with requisite techniques and knowledge.'

Every learning sequence should culminate in a moment of fading that allows pupils to put their new learning to practice, as well as consolidate past learning. An easy and consistent method for planning fading into the end of every learning sequence is through extended writing tasks. Pupils respond to a question in their books and are told they must not raise their hands to ask questions but instead must work through the written task independently. The logic of enforcing 'no hands up' is simple: before setting pupils off on this task, you should have provided enough modelling and scaffolding for them to now be attempting this alone. Hands will be going up for questions like, in my experience, 'Should I leave a line between answers?'; 'Is it OK if I forgot to draw a margin?'; or even 'Can I turn the page now that I've filled it with writing?' (All genuine questions I've been asked, the answers to which, respectively, were 'Yes', 'Yes', and a sort of strangled, exasperated noise of disbelief.)

By having pupils simply get on with writing, you are fading in a way that teaches them to rely on their own knowledge and do their best to work through any obstacles they might encounter on the way. Have pupils underline spellings or workings-out they are unsure of, and then carry on with their work. They will get into the habit of looking for solutions themselves, continuing writing without excuses or constant seeking of affirmation from you, and turning to the next page with gleeful abandon. You are thus free to circulate during the extended writing time, reading over shoulders and identifying any misconceptions. Noting these down in a notebook or scrap of paper will also enable you to check that your fading was timely, and whether you need to reteach any content. Underlining spellings or other content they are unsure of also means that when you read their work, you are able to quickly identify whether an error is due to a pupil's uncertainty, or if they are quite certain that that is how 'repetition' is spelled or when the Battle of Waterloo was fought. This also helps to snap pupils out of the habit of freezing at the first uncertainty, and instead encourages them to work past it.

Considering fading when planning five-year curricula minimises wasted learning and ensures that you have spaces to fade out and then back in again throughout a child's academic career. This is the very structured fading out that occurs on a pre-arranged date and follows a set layout (exams; when a topic should be finished; which topics should be revisited). Considering fading across a term involves considering the essential knowledge needed, as well as opportunities to implement it in weekly tests and termly assessments. This is the fading that is slightly more adaptable: it includes lower-stakes tests and revisiting and reteaching ideas if they are not properly remembered.

Fading within individual lessons is where the real joy is evident – where you can share your love of your subject and give pupils everything they need to find patterns, seek knowledge and experience a hundred small successes every day. Fading is the moment in which you are present but get to step back and watch pupils take their first flight. It's a thrilling moment in teaching. In that sense, 'fading' is a somewhat misleading term – it suggests a certain passivity or something weakening. In fact, it is the moment that pupils truly show their strength, and when teachers get to reflect on just how exciting their job can be.

References

Dixon, R. C., Carnine, D. and Kameenui, E. (1993) 'Tools for teaching diverse learners / using scaffolding to teach writing', *Educational Leadership* 51 (3) pp. 100–101.

Fisher, D. and Frey, N. (2010) *Guided instruction.* Alexandria, VA: ASCD.

Goldstein, E. B. (2011) *Cognitive psychology: mind, research and everyday experience.* 3rd edn. Belmont, CA: Wadsworth Cengage Learning.

Larkin, M. (2002) *Using scaffolded instruction to optimize learning.* Arlington, VA: ERIC Clearinghouse on Disabilities and Gifted Education.

Mastropieri, M. A. and Scruggs, T. E. (1994) 'Text versus hands-on science curriculum: implications for students with disabilities', *Remedial and Special Education* 15 (2) pp. 72–85.

Quinn, D. (2017) 'Never let me go', *Until I Know Better* [Blog], 31 May. Retrieved from: www.bit. ly/2Zb9Llz

Van de Pol, J., Volman, M. and Beishuizen, J. (2010) 'Scaffolding in teacher–student interaction: a decade of research', *Educational Psychology Review* 22 (3) pp. 271–296.

Author bio-sketch:

After completing her master's degree at the University of Exeter, Sarah Cullen joined Teach First for two years before working at the Michaela Community School, where she was Second in Charge of the English department. She has also taught in India and Norway and now works in the British Vietnamese International School in Ho Chi Minh City.

USING DIRECT INSTRUCTION TO TEACH WRITING: SECONDARY ENGLISH

BY AMY COOMBE AND LIA MARTIN

When it comes to teaching writing in a secondary setting, there are a number of direct instruction programmes available that hugely improve students' accuracy. Engelmann's Expressive Writing is just one example of these and is used in some UK schools already. At Jane Austen College, one of East Anglia's Inspiration Trust schools, we use the programme with our Year 7 cohort to ensure that every student acquires a base level of written accuracy before progressing in the school.

It becomes much harder to use direct instruction to teach specific types of writing – analytical, persuasive, descriptive and so on. Because of the nebulous nature of English, and its many component parts (in which content is hugely varied depending on genre and text), it would be impossible to design a do-it-all DI programme for writing as a whole, to be rolled out across the country with structured teacher explanations. We can, however, take the best ideas from DI and apply them to our teaching. The following chapter does not assume that you have hours of time to write, edit, test and re-write perfect DI programmes for all of your writing subjects and their constituent units. We will simply aim to give suggestions that can be incorporated into your teaching right away, as well as some that need more long-term, incremental thinking.

Why do we teach writing using principles from DI?

A common myth, perhaps perpetuated by best-selling books and films on education, is that English teaching is not inspiring enough if it is too teacher-led, replete with quizzing, drilling and controlled questioning. While using DI methods is not the only way to teach English, in our experience, we have found students to be more engaged and motivated by the subject since we have incorporated DI into our practice. Why? Because DI methods help students, even the weakest students, to improve and to feel successful in the subject. It is not enough to be a *Dead Poets Society*-style maverick, endeavouring to spark creativity through force of personality alone. And it is certainly not enough for our most disadvantaged children, who deserve the same chances as their more privileged counterparts, to succeed in this challenging, but essential, discipline.

Effective writing is one of the hardest things to teach. It cannot rely on a 'throw lots of things at them and see what sticks' or a 'they will get there if they just practise lots of extended writing' approach. We have tried these tactics. They do not work for every student. Inevitably, the child who has been exposed to five times fewer words than their peers (Rowe, 2008), or the child who takes shortcuts in their writing practice, will not succeed. We are aiming to clarify our instruction and eliminate misconceptions and to avoid low expectations or poor outcomes for children from poorer socioeconomic backgrounds. We are interested in using methods that enable every single student in the room to improve and achieve success. As Engelmann says, 'all children can be taught', and it is our duty as teachers to improve our instruction, rather than assume that it is the child who simply cannot 'get it' (Engelmann, 1992).

What can we learn from DI principles for teaching writing?

The principles from DI have been covered extensively in this book, but the ideas that we have sought to learn from can be broadly separated into four categories, which we will explore more deeply, in relation to teaching writing, later in this chapter:

1. **Mastery:** the DI research suggests that content should be broken down into manageable parts that can be mastered over time through multiple revisits. For mastery and fluency, Engelmann (1992) suggests that students need five times more practice than most teachers expect. This means building in plenty of discrete practice writing exercises throughout the curriculum. We also want to teach the highest utility content for retention. In writing, this can be applied to how we teach vocabulary, grammar, sentence structure and even how we plan extended responses. We are advocates of methods from Hochman and Wexler's *The Writing Revolution* (2017) and discuss our top practice exercises, and how they relate to DI, later on in this chapter.

2. **Clarity:** if we want students to deeply understand what they are learning, they need to understand teacher instructions with crystal clarity. This has led us to think about the language and examples we use. Are we using too many abstract words? Are we being as clear and concise as possible? Are we using the same wording for instructions so that students know exactly what we mean and know exactly what to expect? How can we get closer to achieving 'faultless communication' in our teaching?

3. **Modelling:** students, particularly novice learners, need explicit instruction in the form of worked examples and teacher-led models. This is especially crucial in writing, a deceptively complex task which can easily overload students' limited working memories. We have tried to incorporate these ideas, particularly live modelling and comparing worked examples (weak, good and better).

4. **Responsivity:** A core principle in DI is rapid, responsive correction of student misconceptions. As well as teacher responsivity, students should play a highly active role in the lesson. Fast-paced questioning and continuous checking for understanding inform how we teach writing.

Applying the principles of DI to the teaching of writing about GCSE texts

1. Writing mastery

Much of our thinking this year has been dedicated to breaking down the writing process into manageable parts and allocating large proportions of lesson time to writing practice. Drawing carefully upon the years of research carried out by Judith Hochman and Natalie Wexler (2017), we have instigated our own 'writing revolution', transforming the way we teach writing to focus less on multi-paragraph compositions and more on sentence-level activities, in order to ensure that the foundations are secured. Not only does this approach set out to develop students' writing skills, but – importantly – the activities are rooted in a secure knowledge of the content the students are being taught. The aim is to advance the students' critical thinking about the content they are being taught while also developing their writing skills. In doing so, we have also been able to address our students' common pitfalls: using stock sentence starters such as 'Evidence to support this includes…'; following formulaic structures such as PEELAC that limit students to one piece of 'evidence' per paragraph and promote a tag-on approach to \ contextual information; and, finally, starting sentences in repetitive and unsophisticated ways, such as 'This shows…'.

A strategy from *The Writing Revolution* that we often draw upon is sentence expansion. Rooted in the same principles as Lemov's (2016) 'The Art of the Sentence' strategy, the approach advocates a belief that a sentence is a very complex thing, the mastery of which is often overlooked. To effectively support students in writing multi-paragraph compositions, we must unlock the mystique by explicitly teaching carefully crafted sentences as the micro-components of good writing. The sentence expansion strategy takes many formats, applicable depending on the content being taught and the aim of the lesson.

Example 1: Turning fragments into sentences

This strategy proves particularly useful in facilitating a more intuitive application of different sentence structures. It also helps students to avoid one of the aforementioned pitfalls by learning how to embed quotations from the text into their sentences.

This example is taken from a lesson in which an extract from *Romeo and Juliet* has been taught. The aim is for students to apply their understanding of Shakespeare's presentation of the overwhelming power of love by expanding a small part of a sentence into a full sentence using the knowledge they have learned.

Example fragment: 'uses imagery of the heavens to'

Turned into a sentence: 'Shakespeare uses imagery of the heavens to suggest that Romeo idolises Juliet as if she were a goddess.'

1. 'makes clear that Juliet values'

2. 'orders Romeo to "deny"'

3. 'is willing to abandon the Montague name in order'

4. 'claims he will be "new baptised" as "love", which'

5. 'makes clear that both Romeo and Juliet are willing to'

Example 2: Sentence expansion using when/who/what/how/why

This strategy explicitly teaches students how to plan a more carefully structured sentence. The planning stage in this activity is just as important as the writing stage. We often find that students forget the writer when analysing literary texts. Using the 'who' question in a sentence-level task explicitly teaches students to internalise their understanding of the text as a construct, and the characters' actions/speech as ideas that have been carefully woven together by the writer. Selecting a quotation when explaining 'how' a writer has achieved an intention explicitly teaches students to embed quotations within a sentence, rather than falling into the common pitfall of beginning a sentence with 'A quotation to support this is…'. We aim to limit the number of questions to three or four in order to avoid overload and overly complex sentences that lose their precision.

Whereas previously we may have planned a PEE paragraph in response to the question 'How does Shakespeare present the theme of fate?', instead we focus on a sentence-level task with very explicit parameters. In this example, we selected 'Who', 'When' and 'How' as the explicit parameters for the sentence.

Write a sentence explaining how Shakespeare makes clear that Romeo and Juliet are fated to die.

Model: He makes clear that Romeo and Juliet are fated to die.

Who? Shakespeare

When? opening prologue

How? lovers = 'star-crossed' and 'death-marked'

Expanded sentence: In the opening prologue, Shakespeare makes clear that Romeo and Juliet are fated to die by describing the lovers as 'star-crossed' and 'death-marked'.

Your turn, with a different example from elsewhere in the play: He makes clear that Romeo and Juliet are fated to die. (NB: this part of the sentence must be used **exactly**)

Who? ....

When? ....

How? ....

Expanded sentence: ....

....

....

2. Explanation clarity

Hand in hand with our approach to teaching the micro-components of good writing more explicitly has been an attempt to be much leaner and clearer in our explanations. Inspired by Peps Mccrea's Memorable Teaching (2017), we have asked ourselves at every opportunity: What is the least I need to say, write or draw for my students to get it? Having this question at the forefront of every pre-planned definition or explanation helps us to try to achieve the optimum level of clarity and simplicity. Not only does this assist us in securing better immediate understanding of tricky concepts, but stripping away unnecessary complexity and detail allows more time for mastering the content.

Example 1: Choosing the modality through which we introduce new content

When reviewing our teaching of poems from the 'Power and Conflict' anthology this year, we tried to apply Peps Mccrea's principles, also drawing carefully on what we know about cognitive load theory. Previously, a first reading of 'The Charge of the Light Brigade' would have been preceded by the teacher reading from three PowerPoint slides, containing contextual information about Tennyson, the poem and the Battle of Balaclava.

This year, we changed our approach. The example below, from our new writing booklet, simplifies the first explanation of what the poem is about and replaces the slide's lengthy descriptions with two images. The aim was to make the first explanation of the poem leaner and clearer, and to recognise that you cannot overload students with too much information too early. We want to guarantee students a basic understanding of the poem's premise before examining it more closely.

Task 1: Read the poem for the first time with your teacher. The poem is about a brave but disastrous British charge against the Russian enemy.

Before reading the poem, we would give a simple summary of it: 'The poem is about a brave but disastrous British charge against the Russian enemy.' After reading the poem, we'd refer back to the images and discuss the Russian soldiers fighting with their 'sabres' (swords) in the left-hand image. We would discuss how exposed the soldiers were to the dangers of battle, charging forward on horseback. In the right-hand image, we'd discuss the lines from the poem 'Cannon to right of them / Cannon to left of them / Cannon in front of them', and how we can see from the image that the soldiers are surrounded by gunfire. This would lead into a short explanation of the context: how a commanding officer 'blundered', sending the brigade into the wrong area, resulting in them being woefully unprepared and extremely vulnerable to attack. We would briefly discuss how the images bring to life the danger, sights, sounds and action of the battle, mirroring Tennyson's intention in his poem.

Example 2: Vocabulary definitions

Years ago, before discovering Beck et al.'s *Bringing Words to Life* (2013), we might have introduced vocabulary by asking students if they know a word. For example, in a lesson on 'The Charge of The Light Brigade', we might have asked a class 'Who knows what the word "patriotism" means?' Five minutes later, after several incorrect guesses, the students would be no closer to an accurate definition and many would be lost in the misconceptions proposed by others in the class. Instead, we now always provide students with the definition of a new vocabulary word, whether we are teaching it implicitly (to quickly aid understanding) or explicitly (investing time for thorough mastery and understanding). Choosing the clearest definition of the word involves careful consideration. For example, when searching the word 'patriotism' on Google, the following definition is offered: 'the quality of being patriotic; devotion to and vigorous support for one's country'. Providing this definition to students relies on them understanding the abstract idea of a 'quality' and requires an understanding of the words 'devotion' and 'vigorous'. As the intention is not to introduce the words 'quality', 'devotion' and 'vigorous', a simpler definition is needed. The 'learner' definition on www.collinsdictionary. com provides something clearer: 'Patriotism is love for your country and loyalty towards it.' However, there is still a question mark around the word 'loyalty', which detracts from the aim to simply focus on patriotism. Another search brings up the 'learner' definition on www. dictionary.cambridge.org: 'the feeling of loving your country more than any others and being proud of it'. This is our favoured definition and we simplify it to 'love and pride for your country'. We will often write our own definitions that amalgamate ideas found on different websites if we don't find a satisfactory definition. When introducing the word to students, we give the definition plus a few examples of what it would mean to be patriotic in order to assist in clear understanding of the word:

New vocabulary: **patriotism** = love and pride for your country.

- If I were wearing a hat that was covered in the UK flag, you might describe me as **patriotic**, as it's clear that I am very proud of my country.

- When we all come together to sing the national anthem, it feels **patriotic**, as we are celebrating the Queen and our country.

- Tennyson promoted the idea of **patriotism** through his poem.

As well as showing examples of the word and its different forms (patriotism, patriot, patriotic), it is important to show incorrect examples of the word's usage, or try to pre-empt misconceptions. For instance, students often mistakenly swap 'patriotic' for 'patriarchal' in their writing, so it is useful to provide an example of 'patriarchal' in contrast to 'patriotic'.

With principles of Direct Instruction in mind, we would ensure that we ask students to practise using the new word, both verbally and in writing. Choral response is useful for checking for pronunciation; asking them to write a sentence using the word is also very important, as well as revisiting the word multiple times in future lessons and explicitly challenging them to use it in their responses. It should be noted that asking students to practise using a word in their writing works best when they are guided to write a sentence that is rooted in the content – e.g. 'Now that you know what patriotism means, write a sentence explaining how Tennyson promotes a feeling of patriotism in his poem.'

3. Modelling:

Modelling – live and using pre-prepared examples – is integral to the success of Direct Instruction methods. When live modelling, we draw upon *Practice Perfect* editor Doug Lemov's 'I, we, you' approach.

In the 'I do' step, we begin by delivering and modelling the process we want students to learn as directly as possible, walking our students through examples and applications.

In the 'we do' step, we first ask for help from students at key moments and then gradually allow them to complete examples with less and less assistance on more and more of the task.

In the 'you do' step, we provide students with the opportunity to practise doing the work on their own, giving them multiple opportunities to practise.

Applying this process helps students because they are able to watch and listen to experts as they guide them through the task, step by step, before they make an attempt themselves.

A strategy that we are particularly excited to be trialling at the moment is a live paragraph model with students actively participating at every step. Deploying Lemov's 'Everybody Writes' idea, we have been asking students to write up a paragraph sentence by sentence, pausing after each one to project an example from the class on to the board and re-work it with student input before asking students to re-draft. We try to avoid split attention by ensuring students are solely focused on the board with their pens down while going through the editing process. Here is a general idea of how this looks:

1. Draft: everybody writes a sentence
2. Display: ask for a sentence from the class
3. Redraft: improve the sentence while all students watch
4. Draft: everybody writes their second sentence
5. Display: ask for a sentence from the class
6. Redraft: improve the sentence with class input

4. Responsivity

Fast-paced questioning and continuous checking for understanding inform how we teach writing. Learning from strategies used in Engelmann's writing programme 'Expressive Writing', this year we introduced choral response into our lessons. Combined with a short recap quiz, this can be an effective way to quickly pick up on misconceptions and address them in the moment. This example is taken from our writing booklet for Act V of *Romeo and Juliet*.

Recap:

1. List three things that Friar Laurence does in an attempt to help Romeo and Juliet.
2. Why does Friar Laurence help Romeo and Juliet to marry?
3. What does Friar Laurence say to Romeo, warning him not to rush? 'They stumble...'*
4. What is Shakespeare foreshadowing when he has Friar Laurence say those words?
5. Which words from the prologue warned the audience of the tragic ending? 'D____-m____ l____'*

*Understanding of the starred questions could be checked using choral response – for example:

Teacher: 'What does Friar Laurence say to Romeo, warning him not to rush, everybody?'

Students: 'They stumble that run fast.'

Doing so immediately highlights gaps in understanding, which can be corrected immediately, if needed, with further recitation of the specific component of knowledge to make sure their understanding is firm before moving on.

We regularly read[3] samples of student books to pick up on misconceptions and often use quizzing in our re-teaching lessons in order to check if students are firm in their understanding of what we have addressed. Example:

Who does Shelley use as a symbol of corrupt power, and who is he actually criticising?

1. He is using King George as a symbol of tyrannical power and he is actually criticising Ramses II.

2. He is using Ramses II as a symbol of tyrannical power and is actually criticising all Ancient Egyptian pharaohs.

3. He is using Ramses II as a symbol of tyrannical power and is actually criticising the British monarch at the time he was writing (King George).

4. He is using King George as a symbol of tyrannical power and he is actually criticising the churches and other institutions.

Using a multiple choice quiz with some of their misconceptions planted within it helps the teacher to check if the misconceptions have been addressed, or if some students still don't understand. The teacher might follow the quiz with the words, 'On my cue, and not before, raise one finger if you think it's number one, two fingers if you think it's number two, three fingers if you think it's number three and four fingers if you think it's number four. After three, everybody: One...two...three...show!' This quick visual check will reveal any gaps, which can immediately be addressed by the teacher.

Next steps
Sequencing lessons using the principles of direct instruction requires constant review and evaluation. While we have made headway this year, integrating the principles of direct instruction into our day-to-day teaching and making this a norm across all lessons in the English department, we recognise that there is still more work to do. A priority for the upcoming academic year is formative testing. We aim to design multiple formative tests on each main sub-topic that give clear, diagnostic visibility on exactly who has forgotten what. Recap quizzes

---

3. We don't mark books with comments and annotations; we read a sample of student books and collate misconceptions to be retaught.

at the start of lessons will become more strategically planned, ensuring that they give clearer visibility for the teacher. For example, a recap quiz might take the form of a character quiz about one character, such as Utterson in Jekyll and Hyde. This draft test is designed to assess whether or not students have mastered the minimum bar of priority content listed for Utterson in the unit plan.

Extract from character test 1: Utterson

1. **Whose viewpoint is the narrative of the story told from until chapters 9 and 10?** Utterson's

2. **List two things that Utterson enjoys but stops himself from doing.** Going to the theatre / drinking

3. **Why does Utterson stop himself from doing these things?** (Challenge: use the word 'repress'/'repression' in your answer) Because he wishes to follow the strict morals imposed on upper-class gentlemen in Victorian London, repressing his desires in order to maintain a respectable reputation.

With teacher guidance, this can be peer marked. Teachers can use the class scores to address misconceptions in order to ensure that the minimum bar for the character of Utterson is mastered by all students.

Additionally, the sequence of lessons will contain interim tests that sample from the minimum bar of taught content.

Example sequence:

(Vocabulary words are in brackets when they are revisited)
1. Plot & Characters
2. Stevenson and the Victorian context
Vocab: morality
3. Chapter 1
4. Character: Utterson
Vocab: narrative perspective (morality)
5. Chapter 2
6. Character: Hyde
Vocab: imagery (narrative perspective, morality)
7. Chapter 3
8. Theme: Good and evil
Vocab: duality (imagery)
9. Chapter 4
INTERIM TEST 1

10. Setting: London and Soho (revisit description of 'door' in chapter 1)
Vocab: symbolism and reputation
11. Plot: Chapters 1–4
12. Context: Darwin
Vocab: evolution
13. Character: Hyde
Vocab revisit: (morality) (imagery)
14. Chapter 5
15. Character: Utterson / Theme: Mystery and secrets
Vocab revisit: (morality) (reputation)
16. Chapter 6
17. Theme: Morality
Vocab revisit: (morality) (reputation) (narrative perspective)
18. Chapter 7
INTERIM TEST 2
19. Theme: Duality
Vocab revisit: duality
20. Chapter 8
Vocab: foreshadowing
21. Theme: mystery and secrets
22. Chapter 9
23. Character: Lanyon
Vocab revisit: (morality) (evolution)
24. Chapter 10 part 1
Vocab revisit: conflicted (duality) (reputation)
25. Chapter 10 part 2
Vocab revisit: (morality)
26: Character: Jekyll
Vocab revisit: conflicted (duality) (reputation)
INTERIM TEST 3
27. Plot: Chapters 1–9
28. Stevenson's themes and intentions
29–37. Mixing plot, character, theme, author, vocabulary, setting, context, structure and quotation exercises with essay planning and practice

Extract from Jekyll and Hyde interim test 1 (sample of questions)

1. What V_____ describes the era in which Stevenson was writing? Victorian

2. Did people in this society have higher or lower standards of behaviour than we do? Higher standards

3. Did this strict code of behaviour encourage people to improve their behaviour, or to hide their desires and do things in secret? Encouraged them to hide their desires and do things in secret

Scores for a test such as the above can be recorded and tracked centrally, which enables each teacher and head of department to see, at a snapshot, how many students across the year group have mastered 70%+ of the minimum bar of content. For the teacher, this ensures misconceptions are being picked up on and addressed, helping all students in the class master the minimum bar. It also helps the department to identify across the year group where there are students who may need additional support beyond the classroom.

Ultimately, the principles of direct instruction appeal to us because they aim to diagnose problems swiftly, to address these carefully and to allow all students to master what they need to know. We have much more thinking to do if we want every one of our students to succeed in becoming excellent writers, but feel that we are, at least, at the start of the right track.

References

Beck, I., McKeown, N. and Kucan, L. (2013) *Bringing words to life.* 2nd edn. New York, NY: Guilford Publications.

Engelmann, S. (1992) *War against schools: academic child abuse.* New York, NY: Halcyon House.

Hochman, J. and Wexler, N. (2017) *The writing revolution.* San Francisco, CA: Jossey-Bass.

Lemov, D. (2016) *Reading reconsidered: a practical guide to rigorous literacy instruction.* San Francisco, CA: Jossey Bass.

Mccrea, P. (2017) *Memorable teaching: leveraging memory to build deep and durable learning in the classroom.* Scotts Valley, CA: CreateSpace Independent Publishing Platform.

Rowe, M. L. (2008) 'Child-directed speech: relation to socioeconomic status, knowledge of child development and child vocabulary skill', *Journal of Child Language* 35 (1) pp. 185–205.

Author bio-sketch:
Amy Coombe teaches English at a secondary school in Norwich. Lia Martin is joint head of English at a secondary school run by the Inspiration Trust.

HOW DIRECT INSTRUCTION CAN IMPROVE AFFECTIVE FACTORS

BY SARAH BARKER

Dragging yourself out for a run is difficult. It's almost entirely a case of mind over matter. From getting on the trainers on a wet November evening – knowing that you still have work to do and food to cook and people who need your time and energy – to the last gruelling mile before the finish, the battle is rarely physical. What motivates runners to do this? Or what motivates the swimmer who gets up at 5 a.m. to be the first in the pool before going on to work a full day? What motivates the cyclist who gets on the bike to do the ten-mile commute, whatever the weather? This question isn't confined to sport; what about the writer, hunched over the keyboard, shoulders aching, eyes stinging, but honing that final draft to perfection? The complicated concept of motivation is crucial to our understanding of success and achievement. How can we motivate our students to challenge themselves and want to keep coming back for more?

When we reflect on the academic success of our students, and consider what exactly contributed to this success, affective factors – such as motivation – are likely to surface as major contributors. While many of us would anecdotally agree that these play a major role in student performance, it is all too easy to dismiss them as beyond our reach and as being solely in the hands, hearts, and minds of our students. In fact, we can harness the positive sides of these variables, and suppress the negatives, to further our students' performance through careful and well-planned instructional methods.

Affective factors can be broadly defined as the emotional factors that impact on human behaviour. These may include, but are not limited to, factors such as motivation and self-concept. For classroom teachers, these may feel like abstract, intangible expanses of psychology, and well beyond the realm of our expertise. Of course, it's possible to work towards improving these areas in the classroom, knowing that these variables will only manifest themselves in the next lesson, or that evening when the student is attempting the homework. Building an understanding of how negative affective factors can be redirected into positives provides an excellent starting point. Coupling this understanding with how Direct Instruction can be used brings about a marked improvement in both affective factors and outcomes.

'Motivation concerns energy, direction, persistence and equifinality – all aspects of activation and intention' (Ryan and Deci, 2000). And, of course, motivation matters because it produces results. Motivation is frequently sub-categorised as 'intrinsic' and 'extrinsic'. As the names suggest, intrinsic motivation is derived from an internal desire to do something, and extrinsic motivation is born out of external factors. Being intrinsically motivated to undertake a task means that a student may be doing it for the sheer pleasure or enjoyment of doing so. The desire to get involved is enough for a student who is intrinsically motivated by a subject. Extrinsic motivation, however, is derived from the pursuit of tangible rewards – such as praise, prizes, or grades. In schools, we rely on our students being extrinsically motivated. We offer rewards for the best (be it 'effort' or 'achievement'). We offer star charts with prizes for completion. We know that our students look to the grade at the end of an assessment before reading the feedback – because securing the grade was the extrinsic motivational factor. Of course, extrinsic and intrinsic motivation can coexist – an athlete who enjoys running may also be motivated by the prospect of the rewards of a race: a medal, or the personal best, or an improved position on the result table.

Some studies have found that extrinsic motivational rewards can cause a decrease in intrinsic motivation, and therefore a drop in desired outcomes. This is known as the overjustification hypothesis, which posits that the delivery of some extrinsic reward will decrease an individual's intrinsic motivation to engage in the behaviour that produced the reward (Roane et al., 2003). Robinson et al. (in press), in an extensive research study into student absenteeism, found that rewarding perfect attendance had a negative impact on attendance. Promises of a reward for good attendance resulted in no impact on attendance figures, and retrospective awards for good attendance resulted in a drop in future attendance subsequent to receiving the reward. The conclusions drawn by the researchers were that rewarding good attendance signals to the families that the school had lower expectations of them, and thus they were being rewarded for exceeding them. When people feel that they have exceeded the expectations for a socially desirable behaviour, they may subsequently become less likely to perform the socially desirable behaviour (Monin and Miller, 2001, cited in Robinson et al., in press). It is to this end that Daniel Pink (2011, quoted in Didau, 2015), argues that 'extrinsic rewards essentially lead to short-term thinking. They act to snuff out intrinsic motivation, diminish performance, crush creativity, and encourage cheating, shortcuts and unethical behavior.' Some meta-analyses show less of a negative impact of extrinsic motivators; but even in these, a negative effect of tangible rewards 'simply for doing a task' are seen.

Fostering intrinsic motivation

Several large-scale studies have shown that intrinsic motivation does not predict academic achievement. Rather, academic achievement is a predictor of motivation (Garon-Carrier et al., 2016; Bouffard et al., 2003; Boggiano et al., 1988; Gottfried, 1990; Harter, 1981). It seems to be the case that we can nurture intrinsic motivation if we create the right conditions. In their expansive work on self-determination theory, Ryan and Deci (2000) identify 'competence' as a vital factor for intrinsic motivation to flourish. Students' positive perceptions of their own competence within a domain are 'motivational precursors of achievement outcomes, including school performance ... and educational choices' (Nuutila et al., 2018). Thus, if we want to create the right conditions for our students to be intrinsically motivated, we need to nurture a sense of self-confidence and competence in them. We know, as a starting point, that our students possess less knowledge of our subject domain than we do. As teachers, we have complex and extensive schemata, while the students – who are undeniably novices – need modelled and scaffolded support to make the links and connections within (and between) domains. Positive self-perceptions of competence, and arguably intrinsic motivation, can be fostered within domains through Direct Instruction as a teaching method.

Project Follow Through, the largest and most expensive piece of educational research ever conducted, evaluated the success of numerous educational models in order to identify the most effective and improve the education of those living in poverty in America. Project Follow Through had three fundamental aims: to increase basic knowledge and skills, to improve cognitive and problem-solving skills, and to promote positive self-concept among the participating children. The results of Project Follow Through were striking: Direct Instruction had the most impact on outcomes across the board – including in affective scores. Explicit instruction, a teaching technique incorporating many elements from Engelmann's Direct Instruction (Rosenshine, 2012), can be applied similarly not just to improve student learning, but to boost motivation. Below are a number of examples of its implementation.

The daily review

Starting with a review of previously learned material is a crucial part of improving confidence and competence and thus develops motivation. Examples could include reviewing a key vocabulary list, or events in a play, or formulae. It's important that the content is being recalled from memory, without the notes or materials from the previous lesson, because simply re-reading notes is an ineffective strategy for revision (Brown et al., 2014, pp. 1–45). The process of retrieving previous learning is achievable, and accessible, and immensely satisfying. It strengthens students' memories and is an excellent starting point in a lesson for developing the sense of competence. Retrieval practice could include:

- **Brain dumps:** Ask your students to write down everything they know about an element of previous learning. After spending five minutes on this, they should check their work for accuracy by comparing what they've written with their notes or resources from the relevant lesson.

- **Think-pair-share:** Pose a question related to previous learning. Give your students a few minutes to think about it. They can then turn to a partner to discuss their ideas. The pairs then feed back to the class.

These methods bring about a sense of achievement and a developing sense of competence. Any inaccuracies in the recalled concepts can be quickly addressed; it's a low-stakes process. Building this into our teaching routine can bring about enhanced self-confidence and motivation. The students need to be well prepared for this, and the demands need to be accessible. Over time, the level of challenge can be increased as confidence grows.

The path to automaticity: present new material in small steps

Developing automaticity is imperative in the pursuit of mastery. That is, we need our students to develop the confidence to handle concepts and processes in our subjects so that they can build on their existing knowledge without *laboured* thought. For example, as an adult reader, you have developed automaticity in reading and writing. You do not need to pause and exert effort to parse or produce every word; it's an automated process. The same will be true of your subject domain; there are fundamental concepts that you know so well – so fluently – that they're there as a base on which you can build your more advanced analyses. For our students to gain self-confidence, in order to promote a love of the subject and intrinsic motivation, we need to get them on the same path. Developing automaticity with the fundamentals needs to come first, and only then will our students have the capacity to delve into the detailed, enriching content of our subject areas. A lack of automaticity in the basics, such as parsing a text, is a stressful experience.

It's crucial to recognise that our students, as novices, do not have the mastery of domain-specific concepts. It's impossible for us, as teachers, to return to the state of 'not knowing'. We cannot possibly empathise with how it feels to *not know*, so we need to plan how we introduce new material with acute awareness of the gaps in knowledge, and the limited automaticity, which our students hold. They do not have the capacity to handle large amounts of new information in their working memories. This means that we need to present new material in very small doses, and avoid any rushed judgements about what our students already know.

Whether we are introducing new concepts, or methods, or vocabulary, we need to ensure we're working slowly, dedicating as much of the lesson as is needed to the new material. Practice is vital at this stage too.

If we take the time to slow down, and break down the concepts into manageable steps, then our students will develop a deep, crafted knowledge and understanding. We're giving them the opportunity to do this without the overwhelming burden of masses of new information to process. Coupled with effective retrieval practice, they will develop resilience and confidence and find joy in the learning process.

Modelling

Building on the acknowledgement of our students as novices, we have to recognise the support they need in producing well-crafted responses. When a student is struggling to produce a decent paragraph (or to balance an equation, or construct an argument), we need to evaluate whether we've ever actually shown them *exactly what to do.* It is deflating for students to have the knowledge but to fail to produce the desired outcome in the right format. In English, we see this a lot in students' essays; they frequently have an excellent working knowledge of the subject matter, but do not know how to structure an essay. Modelling is a fundamental feature of Direct Instruction and brings about confidence in our students, because we move them from a position of inability to craft, or process, or solve, to a position in which they have a method to work by. We're giving them licence to take, use, and apply our models. It's an enlightening process for them to take their teacher's method and to develop the ability, through practice, to eventually do this independently.

Over the last year, we have developed a whole-school approach to modelling. We use the 'I, we, you' model as a basis for our approach, and faculties have worked collaboratively on the domain-specific design of this. We take the time to discuss and plan how we'll adopt these approaches in each faculty, both in department time and during insets.

The 'I, we, you' approach to modelling is effective because it's a scaffolded approach. It is dialogic and allows the teacher to explain the rationale and thought processes during the modelling. It's relatively self-explanatory:

The teacher models a response, giving an explanation or justification for each stage of the process. The explanation may include the chronology ('Notice how I've written this before introducing that…'), the key points to remember in the process ('Remember that I can find the atomic mass at the bottom of each element on the periodic table'), and any other prompt which highlights why the model works ('You'll notice that I have used the word "source" instead of "text" here because…'). In my own practice, I do several 'I' models before moving to 'we'. Repetition is important.

The 'we' model is dialogic. Here, the teacher and the students build a collaborative response on a similar problem or task to the one in the 'I' model. Using questioning and discussion, the teacher guides the students in their contributions to the model. Questioning can also be used to establish whether the students understand why they have contributed certain elements ('Excellent work. I am impressed with your selection of evidence there. Why did you choose something from the first stanza, as opposed to the last?'). We also use Lemov's 'Right is Right' (2010) – it's so important that students are not exposed to incorrect models.

Following this, the students are now ready to work independently on another task. This may be within the same lesson or over a series of lessons. A previous model from the 'I' or 'we' process can be available to them at this stage.

Moving through these stages sets our students up to feel and believe that they can produce the expected quality of response. This must be underpinned by the required knowledge, or the models will be flimsy and our students will not cope when the scaffolding is removed entirely. With the right questioning, and the tenacity and patience to repeat the models until they stick, this process brings about confidence and resilience.

If we're looking to improve motivation, then we need to start with competence and instil a sense of success in our students. Just as the runner will have increased motivation after a successful run, or a new personal best, so will our students' motivation increase after achieving success. It feels counter-intuitive and it's tempting to introduce additional tangible rewards as motivators, but these are unlikely to yield an improvement in achievement. High-quality, thoughtful, and well-planned Direct Instruction will bring about a sense of achievement, self-confidence, and competence in our student. In turn, they'll start to feel a love of learning, and the desire to learn for the love of learning – which, as we all know, is a beautiful place to be.

Bibliography

Boggiano, A. K., Main, D. S. and Katz, P. A. (1988) 'Children's preference for challenge: the role of perceived competence and control', *Journal of Personality and Social Psychology* 54 (1) pp. 134–41.

Bouffard, T., Marcoux, M., Vezeau, C. and Bordeleau, L. (2003) 'Changes in self-perceptions of competence and intrinsic motivation among elementary school children', *British Journal of Educational Psychology* 73 (pt 2) pp. 171–186.

Brown, P. C., Roediger, H. L. and McDaniel M. A. (2014) *Make it stick: the science of successful learning*. Cambridge, MA: Harvard University Press.

Cameron, J. and Pierce, W. D. (1994) 'Reinforcement, reward, and intrinsic motivation: a meta-analysis', *Review of Educational Research* 64 (3) pp. 363–423.

Coane, J. H. (2013) 'Retrieval practice and elaborative encoding benefit memory in younger and older adults', *Journal of Applied Research in Memory and Cognition* 2 (2) pp. 95–100.

Coane, J. and Minear, M. (2018) 'Who really benefits from retrieval practice?', *The Learning Scientists* [Blog], 6 November. Retrieved from: www.bit.ly/2OY6N01

Didau, D. (2015) '20 psychological principles for teachers #9 – motivation', *David Didau* [Blog], 6 June. Retrieved from: www.bit.ly/2KVCtxR

Garon-Carrier, G., Boivin, M., Guay, F., Kovas, Y., Dionne, G., Lemelin, J., Séguin, J. R., Vitaro, F. and Tremblay, R. E. (2016) 'Intrinsic motivation and achievement in mathematics in elementary school: a longitudinal investigation of their association', Child Development 87 (1) pp. 166–167.

Gottfried, A. E. (1990) 'Academic intrinsic motivation in young elementary school children', *Journal of Educational Psychology* 82 (3) pp. 525–538.

Harter, S. (1981) 'A new self-report scale of intrinsic versus extrinsic orientation in the classroom: motivational and informational components', *Developmental Psychology* 17 (3) pp. 300–312.

Karpicke, J. D., Blunt, J. R. and Smith, M. A. (2016) 'Retrieval-based learning: positive effects of retrieval practice in elementary school children', *Frontiers in Psychology* 7, Article 350.

Kohn, A. (1999) P*unished by rewards: the trouble with gold stars, incentive plans, As, praise and other bribes*. Boston, MA: Houghton Mifflin.

Lemov, D. (2010) *Teach like a champion*. San Francisco, CA: Jossey-Bass.

Nuutila, K., Tuominen, H., Tapola, A., Vainikainen, M. and Niemivirta, M. (2018) 'Consistency, longitudinal stability, and predictions of elementary school students' task interest, success expectancy, and performance in mathematics', *Learning and Instruction* 56 (1) pp. 73–83.

Roane, H. S., Fisher, W. W. and McDonough, E. M. (2003) 'Progressing from problematic to discovery research: a case example with the overjustification effect', *Journal of Applied Behavior Analysis* 36 (1) pp. 35–46.

Robinson, C. D., Gallus, J., Lee, M. G. and Rogers, T. (in press) 'The demotivating effect (and unintended message) of retrospective awards', *Organizational Behavior and Human Decision Processes*.

Rosenshine, B. (2012) 'Principles of instruction: research-based strategies that all teachers should know', *American Educator* 36 (1) pp. 12–19, 39.

Ryan, R. M. and Deci, E. L. (2000) 'Self-determination theory and the facilitation of intrinsic motivation, social development, and well-being', *American Psychologist* 55 (1) pp. 68–78.

Author bio-sketch:

Sarah Barker has been teaching and leading in Bristol schools for the past 14 years. She has just completed ten years as a head of English and is now in her first post as an assistant headteacher. Sarah has completed an MA in Educational Leadership and Management at the IoE. She is interested in whole-school literacy, teacher wellbeing and educational research.

IS THIS RIGHT FOR MY SCHOOL?

BY HANNAH STOTEN

So far in this volume we have seen the evidence in favour of the DI approach, and general principles of its use. Here, we consider its implementation in the primary setting, and focus on implementing a DI programme for mathematics education; but the theory, advice and insight here could easily be extrapolated to implementing a programme of DI in any subject. Implementing a programme for mathematics could take the form of a whole-school approach to promote fluency in number, a one-off project to close gaps across the whole school or to upgrade maths teaching before shifting to a different scheme of work, or a system for interventions for children with special educational needs (SEN). Choosing to implement something like Connecting Maths Concepts (CMC) is radical: with its sequenced core knowledge, whole-class approach to pedagogy, frequent testing and higher than average number of opportunities for overlearning, it is the polar opposite of the kind of primary mathematics education that became mainstream in primary schools since the publication of the Plowden report in 1967 (Ernest, 2002).

My views on the process of implementation are influenced by having worked in a number of organisations outside of education that have been using evidence-informed approaches to organisational change (for example, drawing on research in the field of behavioural science) for a lot longer than schools have, so the approach outlined here may be novel. I will firstly outline the key factors to consider before starting a programme of DI in mathematics. Later in the chapter, I will describe some of the concerns and surprising benefits you might encounter while the programme embeds itself into a school's learning ecosystem. Finally, I will illustrate how features of DI lessons can be used to target aspects of teaching and learning in different subjects and year groups, as well as for teacher training.

The theory of change management I use as the prism through which I view the process of implementation is Lewin's force-field model (Hersey et al., 2012). I would recommend this or similar approaches to change management for implementing any new programme in a primary school lest initial investments in curriculum resources, planning and design be put at risk (Forman et al., 2008). A purposeful approach to implementation is especially important for

DI programmes given what we know of the history of DI implementation as described by Engelmann during the years of Project Follow Through: where schools failed, it was almost always down to deliberately or inadvertently poor implementation rather than the programme itself (Engelmann, 2007). The synopsis of this change management approach that follows – combined with a practical interpretation of how it applies to implementing a programme of DI for mathematics – could also be extrapolated to the implementation of any programme of DI. My insights draw from knowledge of typical day-to-day organisation of a wide variety of primary schools, conversations with mathematics educators and leaders in a range of settings in the UK and globally, and through my personal connections to the Home-Ed community.

The learning ecosystem's capacity to absorb change

The force-field analysis method provides an interesting initial framework for looking at the factors (forces) that influence the likelihood of successful change. These forces are either driving movement toward a goal (helping forces) or blocking movement toward a goal (hindering forces). Examples of driving forces include new personnel, legislation, technology and incentives; examples of hindering forces could be fear of failure, organisational apathy or hostility. In order to effect a positive change in the current 'equilibrium' and therefore give a programme of DI a greater chance of success, there needs to be a purposeful strengthening of driving forces coupled to a weakening of hindering forces. As it is imperative that the mindsets of the staff who will be implementing a programme of DI are taken into account, it should come as no surprise that a healthy workplace culture is key to successful change management (Recepoglu and Recepoglu, 2016; Hinde, 2004). Fundamentally, this is about a tactical and systematic approach to winning hearts and minds and this stage constitutes the first part of a three-step process described by Lewin's model as:

1. Unfreeze: the school has to unfreeze the driving and hindering forces that hold it in a state of quasi-equilibrium.

2. Move: an imbalance is introduced to the forces so change can take place (increase the drivers, reduce the restraints or do both).

3. Freeze: once the change is complete, the forces are brought back to quasi-equilibrium and the state is refrozen (this is when the impact starts to reveal itself).

Before instigating the process of change (i.e. starting the programme), you would need to identify, analyse and evaluate all 'forces' for and against change. Being fully aware of changes that will take place helps to provide clarity during the analysis stage. Generally speaking, the following changes and associated tasks will (need to) occur:

- The mathematics and year group/phase leads will need to perform a curriculum-mapping exercise, in order to align the programme of DI to particular year groups, while also developing a cohort-by-cohort strategy for parts of the national curriculum that are not covered by the programme.

- Teachers' planning will need to switch to reading the scripts and teacher guides in advance, in order to ascertain the how and why of the script's purpose (which is planned at the level of children's thoughts for the entire duration of the lesson).

- Teachers will be teaching from a script during the lesson, making it their own while retaining the key components, core knowledge, explanations and key words and phrases.

- Children will be using a workbook and, in the older year groups, a textbook with the expectation that they will be following the teacher's instructions for the entire duration of the lesson. There will also be an increased expectation of independent work at various junctures that take place in relative silence and that will be self-marked straight away. All children will be expected to listen and follow instructions rather than be offered choices or opt out.

In order to understand how those driving and hindering forces will manifest, it helps to really know staff, cohort history and the extra needs of children who may have individual education plans in place. Further, it is useful to be aware that change in itself is actually quite stressful for those that change is being imposed upon, even if that change is positive, sustainable and leading to more happiness and success for all (Wisse and Sleebos, 2016). Adults and children alike prefer routine, organisation and for things to generally remain the same or familiar (Oreg, 2006); the fact that DI is so very different from what people are used to means that you'd need to be even more careful when introducing it for the first time. On the next page is a summary of some of the driving and hindering forces in a primary school that may be considering implementing a programme of DI:

Driving forces	Hindering forces
• The incentive that DI programmes reduce workload for teachers, allowing them to invest more energy into the teaching	• 'Change-fatigue' in staff
• Experienced staff who understand the link between fluency and problem solving	• System-wide pressure to show significant impact and close gaps within an unrealistically short space of time
• A higher than average number of children who need, prefer and thrive on familiarity, structure, routine, instant positive feedback, clarity of instruction, regular periods to work on their own without being disturbed. These children, some of whom may have SEN, tend to struggle with group work and open-ended tasks.	• Low-level disruption in classrooms
	• Opposition to scripted lesson plans among teaching staff and leaders
	• Children used to being given choice and opt-out
	• Children used to receiving a greater share of attention and who tend to call out or finish the teacher's sentences
• New staff whose ITT has included an extensive induction into evidence-informed approaches to teaching and learning	• Potential for high achieving children to feel thwarted/uncatered for
• A supportive SENDCo	• Lack of preparation for lessons
• Classes that are used to high expectations	• Lack of oversight or systematic approach to staff reflection, development and feedback throughout the process of implementation
• A systematic approach to behaviour management already embedded across the school (centralised detentions, shared positive language for behaviour etc.)	• High staff turnover
• Capacity to provide a 'project manager', usually the subject lead, with time, enthusiasm, planning ability and subject expertise to foresee and innovate solutions as they crop up	

Unfreeze

Once you've weighed up the driving and hindering forces, the usual approach is to start off with an all-staff meeting. However, if there is capacity, you could consider creating a small team of early investigators and adopters who are interested in evidence-informed practice and who can see the wisdom in tackling fluency in a systematic and equitable way; they can be entrusted with the task of helping to iron out problems that may arise. Winning hearts and minds is crucial, and visiting other schools (many secondaries use CMC for Year 7 interventions, for example), reading research tasks, and a discussion group should start to build enthusiasm prior to the whole-school introduction. Here is a synopsis of how the process of what needs to be brought to the attention of staff can be structured:

1. A realisation that many children rely on using their fingers to count, for example, and how this makes them both self-conscious and more likely to make mistakes

2. The fact that research shows lack of fluency in number stops children from being able to problem-solve due to cognitive overload (Shoenfeld, 1992)

3. A realisation that planning and creating resources over and over is inefficient and that this energy and time could be better spent on a) teaching and b) work-life balance

4. That the ideal of a perfect sequence of lessons that is planned at the level of guiding children's thoughts includes exactly the right amount of practice at exactly the right intervals and deals with all possible misconceptions before they arise cannot be created by one teacher alone

5. That ad-libbing with the habit of getting into a conversation with various children risks giving more attention and time to the highly articulate, confident and forthright 'haves' at the expense of the 'have-nots' – the remedy here is to assimilate the discipline of giving all children, particularly the 'have-nots', a chance of success

6. That there is an evidence-informed, proven programme of mathematics instruction which is planned to the level of children's thoughts, comes with a script and not only enables high levels of fluency for all but actually teaches them to problem-solve as well, while *reducing* workload for staff

Once staff start to understand the case for DI, it is important that they are introduced to and understand the core principles of DI and how the use of a script provides all this (Engelmann, 2007):

1. Core knowledge/content should be presented without any extra, distracting language.

2. Over-learning opportunities should be abundant.

3. The use of repeated, familiar phrases and key words allows the lesson to proceed with pace and rigour while dialling down cognitive load. This enables pupils to focus on understanding and learning the core content rather than having to decipher what the teacher is saying.

4. 'Wow starters' are best avoided, or re-deployed to the end of a sequence as a 'carrot'.

5. A high percentage of tasks should involve the group responding, rather than individuals – the teacher must be finely tuned to

pupils' responses and stop copying taking place (which manifests as elongated, droning replies).

The other part of the introduction is pre-empting and then allowing those concerns and queries to be aired. Whenever I talk about DI to anyone, whether they work in education or in other industries, the immediate concern is that a script would stifle the teacher's autonomy and creativity in their own classroom and turn them into 'robots' complete with monotone delivery style. There are two ways to deal with this.

The first is to highlight how actors read from a script and make it their own through delivery style; therefore, teachers can do the same (Commeyras, 2007). The seasoned DI teacher will be the one who has progressed from becoming familiar with the script, developing lessons that proceed with pace and rigour, through to being able to see and respond to all the micro-reactions of all the pupils all the time; their class becomes the most fine-tuned of learning ecosystems.

The second way to deal with the 'robot' question is to deal with the real concern that pupils won't listen or pay attention (and will therefore become disruptive) when a teacher reads from a script, especially if it is read in the imagined robotic way. It is this fear of how pupils will react that drives staff apprehension towards scripted programmes. This is because when faced with pupils who lack the ability to automatically listen and pay attention, teachers might assume that pupils are 'not ready' and then make the choice to adapt their teaching style rather than hold their ground so that pupils adapt to the higher expectations instead. Problems can occur when teachers develop a teaching style that is dependent on a type of 'discovery questioning'. The key feature of discovery questioning is that its primary purpose is to mitigate for lack of listening and attention by continuously giving pupils options to almost second-guess what is being taught. This can take the form of asking children whether they already know about X piece of knowledge before actually teaching it, or through a more subtle means of presenting a successive pattern throughout an input and then repeatedly asking children to work out the pattern and make the connections themselves. At surface level, this may look and sound great, but the upshot is that as the teacher adapts to use discovery questioning as a way of gaining attention, so the children will adapt to expect it. At-risk children are left behind because they cannot make connections in the same way and become increasingly frustrated (Parks, 2010). Further, children in this situation also risk developing the habit of calling out, guessing and finishing the teacher's sentences in order to receive as much attention and praise as those who know and can make the connections easily. If the class and the teacher have adapted in this way, then the use of a scripted programme will be more difficult at first, but ultimately its use will lead to a re-adjustment that puts pupils on the path to enhanced listening and attention skills – as well as less exhaustion for the teacher.

If you look closely at the script in a DI programme such as Connecting Maths Concepts, you will see the use of questioning in the DI script is traditional and explicit: knowledge is taught and rehearsed in carefully sequenced steps, and questions require children to recall and apply what they have just been taught, rather than make discoveries in their minds. In this way, DI is more equitable in that it gives all children a genuine chance of thinking about and then obtaining the right answer. If staff are maladapted to low-level disruption, then it might be worth asking questions about whole-school approaches to behaviour management, school culture or the offer of SLT support. If you suspect that staff may be uneasy because both they and the children are maladapted, then the best course of action is to reassure them that no one expects implementation to be perfect from the start, that it will take time for both the teacher and children to adjust and that SLT will be on hand to support if things get tricky.

Once staff have been acquainted with materials and core principles, they will benefit from opportunities to practise before the 'main event'. This can take place during INSET or in the staff meeting, taking the form of teachers working in groups and taking turns role-playing as teacher or pupil. The details they will need to start working on (and this needs to be made explicit) are: pace, clarity, timing of pointing (point before speaking), saying the proper wording, incorporating praise, signals to respond, and the efficient and timely correction of mistakes. Many staff also ask for a demonstration lesson; I would just go ahead and do this, warts and all, to show willing and to show that it's OK to make mistakes.

Move

Staff and children need time to get acquainted with and used to the materials. At first glance, the script seems to mandate an awful lot of teacher talk, but when delivered, it becomes apparent that the majority of the lesson is devoted to directing the children to think about, make links with, use and recall core knowledge in a sequenced way. I recommend a small-scale investigation into the number of calculations or questions answered in a MAP exercise book around the middle to end of Year 2. (This could be a task for the pioneer group of teachers) How does this compare with the 60 odd calculations and questions that children complete in lesson 44 of CMC stage C (one of the NIFDI website examples)? Further, there are keywords, symbols, diagrams and phrases that are regularly used in a DI script. The effect of this is to divert cognitive load away from constantly having to work out what to do and instead enable more thought processes to be devoted to the *substance* of the curriculum. Over time and as pupils become used to the script, the lessons become pacier, more efficient.

The second effect of using a script is that lessons become more inclusive as the class is kept together to listen, repeat, recall, calculate and correct their answers as one entity. Your pupils with SEN dramatically improve and this is because the use of a script mitigates for a type of 'Matthew effect' (Stanovitch, 1986) where teachers deviate from their own internal script through using a conversational style of teaching that appeals to the highest attaining children. If a confident, already-knowledgeable, articulate and high achieving child is keen to ask questions during the input and takes the teacher and a small number of children off on an interesting thought-tangent, at the same time other struggling children will be spending precious moments in the lesson wondering what is going on and then forgetting what they've just been taught. They may also become confused, switched off or distracted. The DI script stops this differentiated conversation from happening and instead deliberately gives less confident children more chances to take part (Haydon et al., 2013).

Setbacks are common during the initial few weeks of implementing any change and it is natural to want to assign blame (Ngo et al., 2015). In a school where there is pressure to transform results, this can take the form of blaming other people, or blaming the programme itself rather than accepting that the process of adjustment is difficult, imperfect and can initially look like teaching and learning is getting *worse* (week 5 is a typical crunch-point). I advise that leaders resist the temptation to abandon (parts of) the programme before it has had a chance to embed and then yield results. During those first few weeks of implementation when adjustment is difficult, the programme is vulnerable and if staff (or leaders) start to assign blame, then mindsets will adapt towards looking for evidence to support its abandonment rather than looking for solutions or the first signs of real progress. This is where leaders need to provide reassurance, frequent constructive feedback and assignments through a programme of regular observations that attend to the following DI-specific lesson features:

- Adherence to lesson format
- Use of clear signals
- Pacing
- Mastery teaching

- Quality of reinforcement/praise

- Watching children (n.b. It is imperative that children face the front in order for the teacher to see individuals during the whole-class responses)

- Timely, efficient and effective corrections

- Class set-up/transitions

Within a term, fluency will start to shine through. Because the programme explicitly teaches problem solving, including the comprehension side of exactly how to interpret word problems, children will become better at problem solving; but don't expect it to magically transform SATs results overnight. The real transformation will gradually build and manifest over time, particularly if the programme is implemented well in Reception or Year 1. The main setbacks will mostly be the byproducts of the hindering forces outlined in the table above rather than an indication that the programme doesn't work, which is much more likely given the strength of the evidence base. For example, if there is low level disruption, then the lesson will not proceed with pace and rigour and children will quickly become frustrated, bored and disenchanted. If staff are desensitised to constant change, then they will be operating on the assumption . that this programme will be removed at some point, so will not invest as much effort in its success. If extroverted and highly articulate children are used to dominating the discourse of the lesson by calling out, finishing teacher sentences etc., then they will object to being expected to answer in chorus and in time with others. When faced with these revelations, the best course of action is to stand firm on those higher expectations rather than go back to the status quo. I also recommend devising a metric for measuring pupils' attention during the initial implementation period because this will provide some interesting feedback to both SLT and teachers as to how pupils' scholarly dispositions are developing while the programme embeds.

In addition to regular observations and feedback, leaders need to become aware of overall pace and efficiency of lessons across each year group. This is easily done by simply asking teachers which lesson number their class is up to; if they are not completing one lesson a day, then further investigation can ensue. However, this does not mean that those who are keeping up or indeed leading the way are not in need of further investigation and this is where triangulation with observation notes is important. The project manager will need to a) check they're not skipping through part of the lesson because it seems 'too easy' (a common misconception and response to higher volumes of overlearning) and b) see where teachers have developed strategies to keep the pace and rigour going throughout the lesson. CMC also comes with mastery tests every ten or so lessons and it should be easy enough for teachers to record this information in their markbooks/whole-class feedback notes to bring to staff and pupil progress meetings.

For the member of SLT who is new to DI observation, choosing key lesson features to focus on can become a form of CPD for the observer as well as being useful for providing constructive feedback. Choral response can be an area where unnecessary time is wasted through children dragging out the ends of sentences as a habit that various teachers can 'tidy up' through adding in clicking, or simply stopping the class and asking them to repeat with a little more pace. Teachers do need to see each and every child's face (and the child needs to see the teacher's, particularly if new to English or if they have speech and language needs) in order to continuously assess for learning and ensure that all are taking part. The use of an appropriate timer is also an important feature when children are doing sections of practice and I recommend the use of a laminated card, green one side and red the other, that is flipped when the children have finished a section. This gives a clear visual to the teacher as to those children who might need more support, and gives an indication of the benchmark for fluency as set by the higher achieving children. It is also important that pupils are placed at the 'grade' that is most appropriate for them while also ensuring that, if needed, they have a chance to catch up. For pupils with SEN, I recommend pre-teaching as an entitlement rather than being in a class where a slower pace is expected and everyone gradually falls further and further behind. For those few pupils who are lucky enough to not need as much practice in order to commit knowledge to memory (be careful here: they still need overlearning and should not be allowed to be sloppy with calculations), then the larger primary school could consider a faster-paced set.

A staff meeting after half a term is the perfect opportunity for staff to bring their observations and concerns. Prior to this, I would recommend (just as I would for all new programmes) facilitating rolling opportunities for staff to have time out of the classroom to observe their colleagues teach. This is a great way to foster a collegial spirit, makes staff feel valued and supported and spreads good practice. It also provides an opportunity for the mathematics lead to teach each and every class and to get a real sense of their progress which can then be triangulated with assessment data. If this is combined with the offer of encouraging teachers in year groups to develop a strategy for providing the elements of the national curriculum that are not covered, then this will also go some way to mitigating the feeling of autonomy being curtailed. Concerns may also be raised about how 'samey' the lessons feel; but it's always worth asking staff to put themselves in the shoes of children: many children need, prefer and thrive on lesson structure that is predictable, particularly if their home lives are unpredictable. DI is therefore very good for children with SEMH and ASD because of the anxiety-reducing effects of routine and structure, the very clear instructions and the vastly increased opportunities to receive positive feedback.

Freeze

Once staff and children have gone through that crucial adjustment period and setbacks have been overcome, the lesson pace will, on average, pick up and then stabilise. Granted, the behaviour expectations for DI are much higher; but if the programme is followed properly, children will also develop enhanced focus and concentration in addition to fluency in number and then this will of course transfer to their other lessons. Further, the efficiency of the DI lesson design in terms of ensuring that children are thinking about the (correct) maths for the majority of the lesson is unrivalled – there is so much potential for a primary school to adopt a programme of DI and then half a decade later to be sending up world-class young mathematicians to secondary schools in their area. In order to back up those observations with data, the mathematics lead will ideally need to design, test and implement a numeracy fluency check for every year group. This is because off-the-peg existing year group assessments in mathematics tend to be heavily biased towards shape and space, particularly for the younger year groups.

Opportunities: students, early years & interventions

If you've decided that a programme of DI is not the right thing for your school just now, there are still other possibilities that come to mind when considering the process outlined above: enabling beginning teachers to build their confidence, giving experienced teachers a chance to write up and share successful lessons for knowledge not covered by CMC, providing children in Reception with the same level of instruction in foundation maths as they receive for phonics, and as a way of providing structured interventions for children with SEN.

Teacher training:

It is striking that despite many providers of initial teacher training advocating evidence-informed practice, new teachers are still largely expected to observe their teacher-mentor and then trial-and-error their way through their induction year. Even if beginning teachers know to plan for sequenced delivery of substantive and disciplinary knowledge and are aware of the importance of streamlined transitions, their lessons may still lack clarity and focus. This is because they experience cognitive overload in the same way children do when being asked to think about too much at once: new teachers are mostly thinking about what children are *doing* rather than what they are *thinking* and this is because they have to work harder to ensure children are paying attention and doing what is expected of them (Berliner, 1988). Direct Instruction may be a useful method to stop beginning teachers maladapting towards being occupied with gaining children's attention and engagement over and above the transmission of knowledge. When teaching from a script, the beginning teacher could instead focus on delivery style, presence and using body language while also assimilating words, phrases and techniques (such as choral response) for enabling the understanding of trickier concepts in children's minds. This is analogous to the violinist immersing themselves in the 'scripts' of the best composers in order to then be able to improvise with flair and panache rather than simply watching and trying out a few vaguely memorised motifs. New teachers will also develop a sense of the quantity of retrieval practice that the majority of children need in order to be successful. For experienced teachers who teach in a similar way, there is also the potential of their creating scripts for the delivery of aspects of the national curriculum for mathematics that are not covered, or even for foundation subjects. In this way, they are creating a body of knowledge for effective teaching and contributing to a 'collective memory' rather than letting good practice fade away.

Early Years:

Using a DI programme of mathematics education in Reception and Year 1 would provide the same high level of instruction and practice as the teaching of systematic phonics does and could potentially radically change, for the better, the attainment profiles of at-risk as well as traditionally high achieving groups. I would like to see more primary schools using grade A of Connecting Maths Concepts from the spring or summer term in Reception – if nothing else, because the power of language and vocabulary acquisition that comes from the frequent choral response, similar to an evidence-informed phonics lesson (Blackwell and McLaughlin, 2005), would go a long way to mitigate the ever-increasing speech and language delay we are seeing in our youngest cohorts (Nasen, 2017).

Interventions:

It is not uncommon for a programme such as Connecting Maths Concepts to be used in Year 7 for previously low attaining groups of children and this is why many are led to believe that CMC is *only* useful for interventions. However, use of CMC for interventions delivered by either teachers or teaching assistants will give children the best possible chance of success, not just because of the attention to detailed building of core knowledge and subsequent improvement in fluency, but because the enhanced efficiency of lessons ensures that for any given unit of time, pupils will be closing those gaps themselves.

Bibliography

Berliner, D. (1988) *The development of expertise in pedagogy.* Washington, DC: AACTE Publications.

Blackwell, A. J. and McLaughlin, T. F. (2005) 'Using guided notes, choral responding, and response cards to increase student performance', *International Journal of Special Education* 20 (2) pp. 1–5.

Commeyras, M. (2007) 'Scripted reading instruction? What's a teacher educator to do?', *Phi Delta Kappan* 88 (5) pp. 404–407.

Engelmann, S. (2007) *Teaching needy kids in our backward system.* Eugene, OR: ADI Press.

Ernest, P. (2002) *The philosophy of mathematics education.* Abingdon: Routledge.

Forman, S., Olin, S., Hoagwood, K., Crowe, M. and Saka, N. (2008) 'Evidence-based interventions in schools: developers' views of implementation barriers and facilitators', *School Mental Health* 1 (1) pp. 26–36.

Haydon, T., Marsicano, R. and Scott, T. (2013) 'A comparison of choral and individual responding: a review of the literature', *Preventing School Failure: Alternative Education for Children and Youth* 57 (4) pp.181–188.

Hersey, P., Blanchard, K. and Johnson, D. (2012) *Management of Organizational Behaviour.* 10th edn. New York, NY: Pearson.

Hinde, E. (2004) 'School culture and change: an examination of the effects of school culture on the process of change', *Essays in Education* 11.

Lewin, K. (1951) *Field theory in social science.* New York, NY: Harper & Row.

Nasen (2017) '83.6% increase in the number of pupils with SLCN as the primary area of need', *Nasen.org.uk* [Website], 27 June. Retrieved from: www.bit.ly/2KArgne

Ngo, L., Kelly, M., Coutlee, C., Carter, R., Sinnott-Armstrong, W. and Huettel, S. (2015) 'Two distinct moral mechanisms for ascribing and denying intentionality', *Scientific Reports* 5 (Article 17390).

Oreg, S. (2006) 'Personality, context, and resistance to organizational change', *European Journal of Work and Organizational Psychology* 15 (1) pp. 73–101.

Parks, A. N. (2010) 'Explicit versus implicit questioning: inviting all children to think mathematically', *Teachers College Record* 112 (7) pp. 1871–1896.

Recepoglu, E. and Recepoglu, S. (2016) 'Change process and the importance of assumptions that form the hidden culture of school: a qualitative study in Turkey', *Anthropologist* 25 (1,2) pp. 122–129.

Schoenfeld, A. H. (1992) 'Learning to think mathematically: problem solving, metacognition, and sense-making in mathematics' in Grouws, D. (ed.) *Handbook for research on mathematics teaching and learning.* New York, NY: MacMillan, pp. 334–370.

Stanovich, K. E. (1986) 'Matthew effects in reading: some consequences of individual differences in the acquisition of literacy', *Reading Research Quarterly* 21 (4) pp. 360–407.

Wisse, B. and Sleebos, E. (2016) 'When change causes stress: effects of self-construal and change consequences', *Journal of Business and Psychology* 31 (2) pp. 249–264.

Author bio-sketch:

Hannah Stoten is an evidence-informed educator currently overseeing Reception and Years 1, 2 and 3, plus mathematics across a large school in Norwich. Prior to teacher training, she worked in financial services, specialising in pension fund accounting. She is the author of a blog called *The Quirky Teacher* and is pursuing an MSc in Developmental Science, researching neurological factors associated with the development of ASD in young children.

SPIRALS, STRANDS AND REVISITING: IMPORTANCE OF REVIEW AND MAKING LINKS IN CURRICULAR DESIGN

BY SUMMER TURNER

If curriculum is 'content structured as narrative over time' (Counsell, 2018), this is partly because it is an age-old narrative which, like any great story, repeats and revisits key concepts and ideas until they collect in our memory for eternity. We know that knowledge is fundamental to a school curriculum, but it is how this knowledge is organised that ensures we remember and can make meaning from it, and that allows us to continue acquiring new knowledge (Oates, 2010) and to apply this knowledge successfully. We often refer to these organising concepts and principles as schemata: the mental structures on which we pin knowledge. Knowledge building relies on coherent sequencing and choice. Curriculum design must therefore address two key questions: why that and why then? And the answers should be able to confirm how specific content contributes to the building of schemata and why the process of visiting or revisiting it at that moment ensures it will support pupils to deepen their knowledge and allow them to make the requisite links between this knowledge.

One of the most fascinating aspects of Direct Instruction is the explicit focus on this aspect of curriculum design, where great care is taken to ensure that the content is chosen and sequenced in a way which obviates any confusion or complexity and instead guarantees security of concepts through the quality of the examples used to teach these concepts or generalisations. Whilst DI is often considered to be about management and traditional teaching, the more 'subtle' aspects of the programme involve 'curriculum design and the quality of teacher feedback to students' (Gersten et al., 1986). This focus on curriculum design is in fact essential to the programme because Engelmann's theory of instruction is driven by the idea that the 'rigorous analysis of exactly how curriculum materials should be constructed' (Gersten et al., 1986) is central to helping children to learn.

This focus on coherence within curricular design is crucial not only at the initial stage, when setting out the exact content which will be studied over time but at each level of curriculum design from over-arching ideas through to enactment of the curriculum. Curriculum coherence is tied up with the premise that 'all elements of the system (content, assessment, pedagogy, teacher training, teaching materials, incentives and drivers, etc.) should all line up and act in a concerted way to deliver public goods' (Myatt, 2018). Dylan Wiliam categorises these different elements as the 'intended', 'implemented' and 'enacted' curriculum, where the 'intended' is the knowledge, skills and concepts which pupils should learn; the 'implemented' is the resulting programme of study including schemes of work and lessons; and the 'enacted' is the curriculum within the classroom, particularly the interactions between teachers and pupils during the process of teaching the curriculum. In curriculum design, it is easy for the coherency between these categories to fall short, which can mean excellent intentions for the curriculum which are not realised because of inexpert translation of these intentions into curriculum planning and teaching. Engelmann's programmes provide a useful framework for thinking about what it would mean to develop a closely linked curriculum in respect to these different categories; he takes the intended curriculum and transforms this into sequenced strands of work, focusing then on the transactions between the teachers and pupils to ensure this curriculum is mastered.

Direct Instruction crosses the potential divide between these three categories firstly by asserting that the curriculum should be organised through concepts, both basic and abstract; secondly by being explicit about the particular examples which should be used to illustrate these concepts; and finally by demanding that the methods for teaching these examples advocated within the programme are followed to the letter (Engelmann and Carnine, 2016).

Many curriculum theorists – from Vygotsky through to Bernstein and Young – share a belief that the teaching of concepts, or a curriculum which builds towards conceptual understanding, is one which can be considered 'transformative' because it is this knowledge which allows children to make links between their own experiences and universal experiences, and which 'provides entry into the "not yet thought" as well as the "not yet experienced"' (Rata, 2016). For Rata, the teaching of academic subjects provides a 'pedagogy of conceptual progression' which provides the 'coherent epistemology' which is sought by those constructing curriculum frameworks. The relationship between academic subjects and Direct Instruction is not a straightforward one and is often strained because of a fear that DI over-simplifies disciplinary approaches, but there is an interesting connection between Rata's argument about the way in which we learn and the theory behind DI. If there is agreement about conceptual understanding as a final aim of curricula, then we must confront the discussions about how to reach this final aim – which brings us back to the role of specific components of knowledge and skill which build conceptual schemata. Alongside this we have to consider how to apply this conceptual knowledge, and how curriculum design contributes to effective and deliberate practice of this material.

In Engelmann and Carnine's *Theory of Instruction*, we are introduced to two 'attributes' which sit behind the idea of learning, which is that we have 'the capacity to learn any quality that is exemplified through examples' and 'the capacity to generalise to new examples on the basis of sameness of quality' (Engelmann and Carnine, 2016). This fits easily with existing educational research and tacit knowledge about how we learn, but it is the intricacy of the design when it comes to choosing these examples, as well as the way in which they are introduced, which is provocative.

> Like the constructivist approach, DI assumes that students make inferences from examples that are presented to them. But, unlike constructivism, the theory underlying DI states that learning is most efficient when the examples are carefully chosen and designed. They must be as unambiguous as possible, sequenced to promote the correct inference for learning a new concept, and involve the fewest possible steps to induce learning. (Stockard et al., 2018)

As indicated by Stockard et al., we often introduce pupils to concepts with one or two concrete examples to help them secure the concept, or with a definition of the concept, whereas *Theory of Instruction* and subsequent Direct Instruction programmes are founded on the supposition that we must be introduced to multiple concrete examples and that these have to be expertly chosen and sequenced to avoid misconceptions. In particular, Direct Instruction works on the premise that we cannot make assumptions about prior knowledge and that we therefore must design a curriculum which builds from the ground up, designed for maximum simplicity and 'utility' and 'demonstrated across a range of examples, not through abstract rules'. Gersten et al. (1986) reflect on the fact that 'too often students are drilled on this kind of information in the context of an abstract rule but with little consistent practice'. Consequently DI programmes are designed to meet a curriculum which has deliberate practice, maximum simplicity, and a range of examples sewed into its fabric. The DI curriculum design, rather than the teacher, therefore dictates how and when pupils should revisit and practise material. This is important because it takes away the potential danger of teacher misconception. If we imagine a normal enacted curriculum when a teacher perhaps introduces a concept into a unit of work, they might do this over one or two lessons; teachers would use some formative assessment to judge how pupils have understood this concept and then more often than not would move on, or would determine that the class on the whole had secured this. Ebbinghaus's forgetting curve (Shrestha, 2017) would probably tell us that even those who seemingly are secure with this concept at this initial stage of testing would be unlikely to remember it months down the line. Direct Instruction takes the randomness of this teacher judgement out of the picture, and could potentially be seen as more reliable as a consequence.

Yet, the most notable aspect of the curriculum design which sits behind DI programmes is not simply this almost scientific focus on examples but that the curriculum model is built around a unique structure known as a 'strand curriculum'. A strand curriculum includes fewer units of work which are covered in more depth until mastery is reached. Within Direct Instruction programmes there is a use of a 'tracked design ... in which discrete skills and concepts are taught in isolation but are then brought together in increasingly more sophisticated and complex applications' (Stockard et al., 2018).

In this structure, lessons are shaped around 'multiple skills or topics rather than around a single skill or topic' (Snider, 2004) and each of these skills/topics is attended to for short segments of time (five to ten minutes) and revisited over several days until these discrete skills/topics are mastered, meaning that only about 10–15% of material within a lesson is new material (NIFDI, no date). Historically, designers of curricula have structured them as a spiral, exposing pupils to a number of different topics which are covered at a fairly fast pace and then revisited in following years with the expectation that pupils who initially struggled with the material will pick it up later down the line. For example an English spiral curriculum might include introducing concepts such as metaphor, similes, personification, rhyme and rhythm within one unit of poetry in Year 7, with the expectation that pupils may pick up some understanding of these techniques but that they would need to be re-taught in later years. There has been some criticism of this approach to curriculum design because of a fear that 'either students are exposed to material that is beyond their grasp ... or the material is watered down until it is accessible ... but then bears little relationship to the discipline or the subject' (Wiliam, 2013). Falling academic achievement in US schools, particularly in mathematics, has also caused educators to look critically at the spiral curriculum and instead investigate the strand curriculum which is found in Direct Instruction programmes.

In Snider's (2004) paper comparing the spiral and strand curricula, she notes that research on the spiral curriculum demonstrates that it has led to low pupil achievement because of the 'superficial' way in which topics are taught, the 'inappropriate rate' in which concepts are taught leading to limited 'academic learning time' and 'insufficient cumulative review'. This was supported by research from Schmidt et al. (2002) which found that the countries with highest achievement in maths had a limited number of topics and covered these in greater depth. In comparison, the strand curriculum means that skills and topics are visited frequently in short segments of every lesson over a sustained period of time such as a term, and because of this interleaving there is the opportunity both for mastering these skills and topics, as well as the opportunity to revisit and review prior learning. For example, in the DI programme Expressive Writing, which concentrates on teaching the mechanics of writing, a lesson can include multiple strands of curriculum content. These strands are taught both in small chunks at sentence level and woven together in the final task of each lesson within an extended piece of writing. In the second lesson of Expressive Writing 2 (Engelmann and Silbert, 2004), pupils complete discrete sentence-level activities on the past tense, capitals and periods (full stops), subordinate clauses, fixing run-on sentences and correctly punctuating speech before combining two or more of these to write a paragraph based on a picture storyboard.

In a strand curriculum, such as Expressive Writing, there is a move to focus on smaller sets of concepts in order that these are mastered, and then increase the complexity of these concepts rather than providing challenge by introducing a larger set of concepts at a higher frequency. The thinking behind this is so that pupils remember what they have been taught in the long term, rather than simply remembering the encounter. Snider (2004) looks in depth at the impact of this in the Direct Instruction programme Connecting Maths Concepts (CMC), exploring how the focus on a small set of important concepts 'such as number families, operations with whole numbers, "fractions equal to 1", and using tables to solve a variety of word problems' not only helps to ensure mastery, but also 'promotes the depth of understanding' which allows children to employ sophisticated strategies such as applying the strand of 'fractions equal to 1' to areas such as solving ratio and ratio-table problems.

A challenge posed to advocates of a mastery curriculum is that deciding pupils can not move forward until they have mastered content runs the risk of making learning stagnant; however the strand curriculum alleviates this through introducing different topics at the same time, meaning that the pace of learning is maintained. This is also designed to address the rate of topics being introduced, with smaller and smaller units of time being dedicated to basic concepts in order that more complex concepts can be interwoven into the curriculum. Basic concepts – such as how to ensure simple sentences are correctly punctuated – are visited frequently throughout Expressive Writing, but in small chunks which are eventually brought together with more complex concepts such as punctuating speech. Pupils are therefore encouraged to write more-sophisticated paragraphs without losing the focus on getting the basics right. Ideally the strand curriculum ensures that every child is able to grasp every concept and that there is a high success rate so that complexity is only introduced when it can be mastered by all children. This strand structure is an identifying feature of DI and another example of how the programmes can provide a model for curricular thinking. It is worth evaluating the structure of curriculum to consider how we ensure that skills, topics, concepts are taught at the appropriate rate and frequency that allow all pupils to achieve mastery.

This is not to say that DI is an answer to all curriculum questions, and there are plenty of well-founded criticisms, including some from knowledge advocates such as E.D. Hirsch. Hirsch and Engelmann have a history of critiquing each other's work (Didau, 2016), which comes as a surprise to curriculum thinkers who often look to both experts for guidance. However, Hirsch's criticism is not that DI doesn't work but that it perhaps has limited grounds beyond teaching the 'mechanics' of literacy and numeracy. He concurs with the argument that Direct Instruction and Success for All (both scripted reading programmes) 'succeeded better than more naturalistic approaches in bringing children to elementary competence in sounding out printed text' (Hirsch, 2016). However, he also draws on a 1982 study by Becker and Gersten, which explored the impact of DI for students in 5th and 6th grade. This study found that although those who had studied DI 'still decoded a bit better than disadvantaged children … they could not understand what the texts were saying any better than students who had not had Direct Instruction' (Hirsch, 2016).

Hirsch labels this as 'fadeout' and although he does not argue that there is no room for DI, he does suggest that DI alone is not enough, and he points to the need for a coherent knowledge-rich curriculum to sit behind these methods, in order to drive learning beyond the mechanics of reading. This is a useful criticism when considering the extent to which DI should be adopted as a single curriculum model and points to the need to remember the role of knowledge and subjects alongside the structures and sequence of curriculum.

Yet this doesn't need to undermine Direct Instruction as a programme or diminish the lessons we can learn from exploring its construction. As Tom Needham points out: 'No one, not even staunch DI enthusiasts, is suggesting that scripted lessons are appropriate to teach extended essay responses, literary analysis or other such subjective, deeply complex skills' (Needham, 2018).

In the narrative of curriculum thinking, Direct Instruction is a useful and provocative part of the story and one which deserves our attention.

References

Counsell, C. (2018) 'Senior curriculum leadership 1: the indirect manifestation of knowledge: (A) curriculum as narrative', *The Dignity of the Thing* [Blog], 7 April. Retrieved from: www.bit. ly/2KEr2eW

Didau, D. (2016) 'Hirsch vs Engelmann: "No scientific basis for Direct Instruction"?', *David Didau* [Website], 2 December. Retrieved from: www.bit.ly/2Z0QwvN

Engelmann, S. and Carnine, D. (2016) *Theory of instruction: principles and applications.* Eugene, OR: NIFDI Press.

Engelmann, S. and Silbert, J. (2004) *Expressive writing* 2. New York, NY: McGraw-Hill Education.

Hirsch, E. D. (2016) *Why knowledge matters: rescuing our children from failed educational theories.* Cambridge, MA: Harvard Education Press.

Myatt, M. (2018) *The curriculum: gallimaufry to coherence.* Woodbridge: John Catt Educational.

Needham, T. (2018) 'Insights from Direct Instruction part 1–9', Tom Needham: *Thoughts About Teaching* [Blog]. Retrieved from: www.bit.ly/33MXu6y

NIFDI (no date) 'Teaching to mastery', NIFDI [Website]. Retrieved from: www.bit.ly/2TGmqaU

Oates, T. (2010) *Could do better: using international comparisons to refine the national curriculum in England.* Cambridge: Cambridge Assessment.

Rata, E (2016) 'A pedagogy of conceptual progression and the case for academic knowledge', *British Educational Research Journal* 42 (1) pp. 168–184.

Shrestha, P. (2017) 'Ebbinghuas forgetting curve', *Psychestudy* [Website], 17 November. Retrieved from: www.bit.ly/31HqkTM

Snider, V. E. (2004) 'A comparison of spiral versus strand curriculum', *Journal of Direct Instruction* 4 (1) pp. 29–39.

Stockard, J., Wood, T. W., Coughlin, C. and Khoury, C. R. (2018) 'The effectiveness of direct instruction curricula: a meta-analysis of a half century of research', *Review of Educational Research* 88 (4) pp. 479–507.

Wiliam, D. (2013) Redesigning schooling – 3: *principled curriculum design.* London: SSAT.

Author bio-sketch:

Summer Turner is Director of Curriculum at The Inspiration Trust and author of *Bloomsbury CPD Library: Secondary Curriculum and Assessment Design.*

ALL CHILDREN CAN BE TAUGHT

THE RELATIONSHIP BETWEEN PEDAGOGY, CURRICULUM AND EXPLICIT INSTRUCTION, AND WHY THIS SUPPORTS PUPILS WITH LOW PRIOR ATTAINMENT

BY JOHN BLAKE

Introduction

Much argument in English education is, either explicitly or implicitly, about the children who do not succeed in our schools. The fundamental defining issue of much education policy discussion over the past decades has been on the question of academic selection, at the heart of which sat the question of what happened to those who did not gain access to grammar schools. Notwithstanding government efforts to address, under various titles and guises, the needs of the 'gifted and talented', the 'tail' in English education remains both stark and important (Hutchinson et al., 2018). So anyone proposing a strong frame of curriculum and pedagogy for our schools must be able to provide a robust argument for why and how such frames would work for children who, for whatever reason, are currently lower attainers in our schools. Pedagogic methods focusing on 'explicit instruction', whether tied tightly to a particular programme or applied more generally, must explain how and why they could be considered to work for such children.

Before considering the actual methods used in the classroom, however, it is necessary to answer a wider question, about 'curriculum content'. Attempts to meet the needs of lower attaining pupils offered by educationists of 'progressive' viewpoints often suggest that explicit instruction is insufficiently motivating for young people, denying them agency over their learning, and directing them in such a way as to require them to form particular knowledge, ideas and values – often with the implication that such knowledge is set to fashion young people in ways contrary to their own inclinations, but convenient for the political system in which they live (for example: Johnson et al., 2007).

Therefore, before considering the extent to which any form of explicit instruction as a pedagogic tool might work for lower attaining young people, it is necessary to answer the question of whether any curriculum which such instruction is set to support is appropriate, given that such a curriculum must, of necessity, be tightly defined in its content and objects. In short, if children are not attaining in the curriculum we offer them, should we persist in offering it to them (perhaps using explicit instruction to enhance their understanding), or ought we to offer a different curriculum (perhaps one co-constructed with the young people, or even entirely determined by them)?

What is 'curriculum'?

To address the question of when, if ever, it is acceptable to provide a different curriculum to weaker students, and what the implications of this might be for the pedagogies deployed, it is necessary to first be clear about my own conception of the curriculum. Here, I mean the subjects which are taught in timetabled classroom time. I am aware there are other more expansive definitions of curriculum which encompass the full range of experiences a young person has in school, or indeed in their life more generally. Although I consider that school does have some role as the location in which such experiences might occur – and even as the agent or facilitator of those experiences – I would argue that schools share responsibility for the outcomes of this wider conception of curriculum with other parts of society – families, communities, other agencies of the state, and often young people themselves; indeed, in many cases, it would not be desirous for schools to take full responsibility or even a leading role in fashioning these wider experiences (Blake, 2019).

Therefore, the curriculum I am discussing here is the subject curriculum, what I imagine most parents would think of if you asked them to describe 'the school curriculum': English, maths, science, history, art, music and so on.

This is the most fundamental aspect of curriculum for schools because this is where school has a unique role: only in a school, where learning can be sequenced over weeks, months and years in a coherent and logical way, can young people be given an induction into both the modes of thinking and fields of information – the disciplines – that underlie these subjects.

The role of 'disciplines' in curriculum construction

Why is such an induction important? There are three main reasons to ensure that young people are inducted into knowledge in this way.

In the first case, there is a straightforward instrumentalist case that not building curriculum in this way impairs the life chances of young people, especially the most disadvantaged. Researchers have credibly illustrated that the advantage in life outcomes enjoyed by students who attend selective education, either private or state-provided, is, at least in part, a function of the coherence of subject curriculum they have experienced, and not merely – or not solely – an outgrowth of the social privilege and cultural capacity which is generally assumed to be due to those whose parents can afford a private education (Iannelli, 2013). Equally, evidence suggests competency-based curricula – those that substitute generic concepts such as 'resilience' or 'problem-solving' or which proclaim the value of '21st-century skills' – impair the life chances of working-class young people by trapping them in narrow school-work pathways which they are actively disempowered from being able to challenge for want of a more rigorous education (Wheelahan, 2009).

The second reason goes beyond the individual's life outcomes and considers their role in wider society. In any society, the existence of a common set of cultural markers and conversational touchstones is important. 'Cultural literacy' matters, especially in a democracy, and schools are incubators of this; if they do not act in this way, children from households where such cultural literacy is taken for granted – because their parents received such an education, or because there is time, space and resources available to correct the deficiencies in the school curriculum – can acquire it for themselves, but this is much harder for those without these advantages. Thus, a subject-based curriculum is important for individual cultural literacy as well as wider social justice (Simons and Porter, 2015).

The third argument, which I would consider the most powerful – and indeed, the underlying explanation for the first two points – concerns the nature of knowledge itself. The current state of curriculum discussion in England's schools is the result of a decades-long shift away from the value of knowledge, even whilst the carapace of the national curriculum attempted to enforce it. The idea of teachers as authorities aiming to impart knowledge that was outside the lived experience of the young people in those teachers' classrooms – and that was more important than knowledge which young people had already acquired from their own lives – was rejected. It is easy to mock the results of that trend – the substitution of Mozart for pop artists in music teaching, for example, or English language examinations preoccupied with the construction of commercial adverts instead of Victorian novels – but some care should be taken in doing this. The critique of the curriculum from, say, the 1960s onwards as hidebound and elitist is not adequate, but it is not entirely absurd either. Decisions about school curriculum content were largely the result of tradition rather than conscious and codified thinking, and therefore often reflected the power structures of those charged with making such decisions. The wider subject communities which were the basis for the school subjects were, in an age before mass communications and high university attendance rates, bastions of privilege.

However, whatever the rights and wrongs of such curriculum formation may have been, it was an error to seek to move away from traditionalist conceptions of curriculum content without considering whether the content itself might be viable and valid in some way that went beyond the social circumstances of its creation. Could it be possible that some, if not all, of the curriculum in many subjects was a sensible and worthwhile induction into knowledge that could be, with some adjustment and thought, rested on much stronger theoretical foundations?

Thinking along this line has resulted in the concept of 'powerful knowledge': knowledge about the world and the way that it works – and the way such knowledge is created, curated and challenged – which is valid for everyone, whether they possess the privileges of those who generated the knowledge first or not. Instead of arguing that 'knowledge is power' because it was forged by and reflects the interests of the 'powerful', it is possible to argue that knowledge possesses a character of its own that transcends the petty politics of the moment of its creation. This, it is argued, is because humans have organised knowledge into disciplines, where the knowledge itself – as well as the necessary skills and attitudes towards that knowledge, and the rules and processes for how to acquire and question it – has been codified in such a way that, once inducted into the discipline, anyone can participate (Young et al., 2014).

Rooting school curriculum in the idea of powerful knowledge provides a clear and compelling rationale for both organising the timetable around subjects and conceiving of those subjects as an induction into those disciplines. The correspondence between subjects and disciplines is not always precise: school and academic history align relatively strongly; whilst school geography explicitly draws from physical and human geography, two very different disciplinary animals; and performing arts in school are much more likely to relate to their creative communities than to academic musicology, for example. However, if an adequate description of the external disciplinary community can be created, it is possible to generate the means and methods to create a curriculum bestowed with the authority of that discipline, and responsive to changes and critiques within it. In some cases, the resulting curriculum may look very similar to one designed by those who take only the knowledge hallowed by tradition as their authority; but powerful knowledge is crucially distinct in that its rationale is public, and the rules for its reiteration available to all (Young and Muller, 2013).

Even for young people who do not wish to pursue an academic career – and most of course will not; and even if they did, none will do so in all the subjects they study – powerful knowledge is important because it aims to embed the foundational knowledge necessary to understand the disciplines in later life, whenever and wherever they are encountered – which, given their centrality to wider human knowledge, will be frequently and often in circumstances that are impossible to predict. It is for this reason that whilst powerful knowledge is a strong argument on its own for constructing the curriculum around subjects, it is also the underpinning of both the cultural literacy and instrumentalist argument for a curriculum of this sort.

Relationship of curriculum to pedagogy

If, as I have argued, it is therefore the case that curriculum is an entitlement for all young people, then low attainment cannot be a reason for not pursuing that entitlement for all children. At this point, the question becomes: by what tools might that curriculum entitlement best be achieved?

It is the case that curriculum content and pedagogy do not have to strongly determine each other. For example, even if one wishes to ensure that all young people learn the specified curriculum content, regardless of their prior attainment, one might still advocate the use of open-ended methods of instruction which offered an illusion of agency to young people, but were in fact tightly controlled to bring them to specific knowledge and understandings. To borrow phrases from Basil Bernstein, we might wish to strongly 'classify' knowledge, but weakly 'frame' it. Bernstein defined these as follows:

> Classification ... refers to the degree of boundary maintenance between contents ... Frame refers to the degree of control teacher and pupil possess over the selection, organization and pacing of the knowledge transmitted and received in the pedagogical relationship. (Bernstein, 1971, pp. 49–50)

Arguably, the work of history educators on the use of 'enquiry questions' is such an example. This common method amongst history teachers involves curriculum content being orchestrated by the teacher around a key historical question – such as 'Why did William the Conqueror win the Battle of Hastings?' In this form, knowledge may be relatively weakly framed, with teachers and pupils working together to 'tackle' the historical question in a manner which, in some respects, mimics the behaviour of academic historians going about their research (Riley, 2000, p. 8). However, it is unlikely the teacher in this situation is operating with any expectation that their pupils will genuinely produce a new or original view on this question which has escaped previous historians. Teachers are likely to have a very clear sense of precisely what answer young people ought to conclude at the end of the teaching period – therefore, they have a strong classification of the knowledge. However, the risk run by weaker framing of strongly classified knowledge is that misconceptions creep in, but these are not necessarily identified or challenged because the weaker framing results in them either not being identified or being accepted as part of the process of discovery for young people valued by any weaker framing device.

Explicit instruction and low prior attainment

A distinction between classification and framing is important and useful because it makes clear that a knowledge-rich education does not necessarily require an explicit instruction pedagogy. However, there clearly is a natural affinity between the two, and this is certainly embodied within the most famous of explicit instruction programmes, Engelmann's Direct Instruction (DI). Engelmann, indeed, focused on curriculum as the major cause of student underperformance (for example, his fairly bluntly titled essay 'The curriculum as the cause of failure' – Engelmann, 1993), and proffered his Direct Instruction pedagogy as intimately bound to correcting the failures in both curriculum content sequencing and planning, and the transmission of this knowledge in the classroom.

DI offers an exceptionally tightly sequenced curriculum delivered through clearly prescribed pedagogy in order to both achieve the curriculum entitlement – that is, to strongly classify knowledge – and also to minimise to the smallest possible degree any chance of misconceptions appearing during the learning of such knowledge, but also strongly framing the knowledge. Other forms of explicit instruction exist, and Rosenshine gives a more expansive definition of what 'direct instruction' (without the capital letters, to underline the difference) involves, which is more concerned with pedagogy (Rosenshine, 1976).

However defined, does this fusion of curriculum and pedagogy through a method of explicit instruction actually work for all pupils? Critics of the strong classification and framing of knowledge have, naturally, been strongly critical of explicit instruction, contesting the centrality of knowledge to curriculum, but going further and suggesting that, even were strong classification of knowledge accepted, weaker framing is important because it provides greater motivation to learn, through being more relevant to young people's interests and because of a reduction in teacher exposition (for example, see Watanabe-Crockett, 2019).

The evidence cited by Rosenshine (and that of Project Follow Through, and many other studies in the years since) suggests that this conviction that direct instruction – whether Engelmann's own or any of a wider variety of explicit instructional methodologies – is a barrier to the learning of children with low prior attainment appears to be quite wrong. Indeed, the opposite would appear to be the case.

Conclusion

The abiding problem of English education has been the quest to address the tail of underachievement in our schools. Attempts to address that tail by substituting an alternative curriculum for underachieving young people (that is, alternative to that studied by their peers) may be well intentioned but are, in fact, a denial of fundamental entitlement for those young people. It is not acceptable for some young people not to receive the full range of their entitlement; the knowledge they need ought to be strong 'classified'.

If this is accepted, then how weakly 'framed' ought to be the knowledge young people are confronted with? Is a sense of 'agency' over learning a tool for motivation of young people? And if it is – and the point is contested – does that overcome the risks of misconceptions creeping into young people's mental architecture through such methodology? Indeed, might such misconceptions be one of the reasons that young people are flagged as 'lower attaining' in the first place? And that even when they are taking in new knowledge, it is being stored within a mental architecture flawed by misconceptions, and therefore not useful for building the powerful knowledge they require?

When phrased in this way, the use of explicit instruction – however tightly defined – becomes one of efficacy, not ideology. For those children who are lower attaining, a structured route into knowledge seems a far surer bet than writing the map themselves.

References

Bernstein, B. (1971) 'On the classification and framing of educational knowledge' in Young, M. F. D. (ed.) *Knowledge and control: new directions for the sociology of education*. London: Collier-Macmillan, pp. 47–69.

Blake, J. (2019) 'Is curriculum only what is taught in lessons?', *Ark* [Website], 20 May. Retrieved from: www.bit.ly/2ZiD5qg

Engelmann, S. (1993) 'The curriculum as the cause of failure', *Oregon Conference Monograph Journal* 5 (2) pp. 3–8.

Hutchinson, J., Robinson, D., Carr, D., Hunt, E., Crenna-Jennings, W. and Akhal, A. (2018) *Education in England: annual report 2018*. London: Education Policy Institute.

Iannelli, C. (2013) 'The role of the school curriculum in social mobility', *British Journal of Sociology of Education* 34 (5–6) pp. 907–928.

Johnson, M., Gotch, A., Ryan, A., Foster, C., Gillespie, J. and Lowe, M. (2007) *Subject to change: new thinking on the curriculum*. London: Association of Teachers and Lecturers.

Riley, M. (2000) 'Into the key stage 3 history garden: choosing and planting your enquiry questions', *Teaching History* 99 (1) pp. 8–13.

Rosenshine, B. (1976) 'Recent research on teaching behaviors and student achievement', *Journal of Teacher Education* 27 (1) pp. 61–64.

Simons, J. and Porter, N. (eds) (2015) *Knowledge and the curriculum*. London: Policy Exchange. Retrieved from: www.bit.ly/30hByy9

Watanabe-Crockett, L. (2019) 'Inquiry-based learning vs. Direct Instruction: 7 important differences', *Wabisabi Learning* [Blog], 11 April. Retrieved from: www.bit.ly/2ZeNTBU

Wheelahan, L. (2009) 'The problem with CBT (and why constructivism makes things worse)', *Journal of Education and Work* 22 (3) pp. 227–242.

Young, M. and Muller, J. (2013) 'On the powers of powerful knowledge', *Review of Education* 1 (3) pp. 229–250.

Young, M., Lambert, D., Roberts, C. and Roberts, M. (2014) *Knowledge and the future school: curriculum and social justice*. London: Bloomsbury.

Author bio-sketch:

John Blake is Curriculum Research and Design Lead for Ark Curriculum Partnerships and Director of Policy and Strategy for Now Teach. He was previously head of education policy in a think tank, a senior and middle leader in schools, and a history teacher for ten years.